AN INTRODUCTION TO
PHILOSOPHY OF HISTORY

Philosophy

Editor
PROFESSOR H. J. PATON
MA, FBA, D.LITT, LL.D
Emeritus Professor of Moral Philosophy
in the University of Oxford

BY THE SAME AUTHOR

Reason and Experience
(Clarendon Press, 1947)

Metaphysics
Hutchinson, 1963

AN INTRODUCTION TO PHILOSOPHY OF HISTORY

W. H. Walsh

Professor of Logic and Metaphysics in
the University of Edinburgh

HUTCHINSON UNIVERSITY LIBRARY
LONDON

HUTCHINSON & CO (*Publishers*) LTD
178–202 Great Portland Street, London W1

London Melbourne Sydney
Auckland Bombay Toronto
Johannesburg New York

First published 1951
Reprinted 1953, 1955, 1956
Second edition 1958
Reprinted 1961, 1964
Third (revised) edition 1967

This book has been set in Fournier, printed in Great Britain
on Smooth Wove paper by Anchor Press, and
bound by Wm. Brendon, both of Tiptree, Essex

CONTENTS

PREFACE TO THIRD EDITION

In this enlarged edition the main text appears as amended for the 1958 edition, except for minor verbal changes. A few notes have been added, and these are put in square brackets. The note on books for further reading has been completely revised. But the main change is that, thanks to the generosity of the publishers, I have been able to add two more recent essays in the same general field. 'The limits of scientific history', which was originally published in *Historical Studies* III in 1961 and is reprinted here by kind permission of Messrs Bowes and Bowes, develops points made briefly in my previous Appendix II, now omitted. 'Historical causation', given as a paper to the Aristotelian Society in 1963 and reprinted here by kind permission of the Society, attempts to fill a somewhat serious gap in the previous treatment. Both, as will be obvious, are written with more of an eye to historical practice than was the book itself. If I were to write the book again now I should hope to make this change throughout.

I should like to dedicate the book in its new form to my friend and former tutor in history, Robin Harrison, Warden of Merton College, Oxford.

W.H.W.

1967

PREFACE TO FIRST EDITION

The range of topics this book seeks to cover is the subject of its introductory chapter. To sum the matter up in terms which are convenient if pretentious, Chapters 2–5 may be said to deal with questions in the logic of historical thinking, whilst Chapters 6–8 form a critical discussion of various attempts to arrive at a metaphysics, or metaphysical interpretation, of history. If any reader expresses surprise that matters so different should be treated in a single volume, I can meet him half-way by admitting that I am conscious of the incongruity myself; though I do not feel so clear as I once did that the problems which are touched on in my final chapters are wholly irrelevant to those treated in the earlier part of the book.

To avoid misunderstanding, I should make clear that my primary aim is to write for philosophers, not for historians. It seems to me very odd that teachers of philosophy should with such unanimity expect their pupils to discourse on the logic of the natural sciences and mathematics, with which subjects few of them have much close acquaintance, and scarcely ever ask them questions about the procedures and statements of historians, though in many cases they are students of history as well as of philosophy. If I can show that there are problems about history to which philosophers might well give their attention, I shall have accomplished my main purpose. Naturally, I shall be pleased if historians show interest in what I have to say; though if I am told that my questions are largely, or even wholly, irrelevant to historical studies proper, I shall not count that as a major reproach. Philosophers are notoriously rash men, but I hope I shall not be thought to have the presumption to tell historians how to go about their own business.

It will be obvious how much I owe to Collingwood, though I have tried not to follow him wholly uncritically. I have also learnt a lot in discussion with Mr P. G. Lucas, of the University of Manchester, who read early drafts of four of my first five chapters, and whose comments drew my attention to some shocking simplicities of thought. He must not be blamed for those which remain. I should like to thank him and also Prof. Paton, who read the whole book in typescript and saved me, among other things, from a bad blunder in Chapter 6.

W.H.W.

December, 1950

I

WHAT IS PHILOSOPHY OF HISTORY?

§ 1. *Current suspicion of the subject*

A writer on philosophy of history, in Great Britain at least, must begin by justifying the very existence of his subject. That this should be so may occasion some surprise; yet the facts are clear. No philosopher would dispute the assertion that there is a fairly well-defined group of problems which belong to the philosophy of the physical sciences, and which arise when we reflect on the methods and assumptions of those sciences, or again on the nature and conditions of scientific knowledge itself. Philosophy of science, in some sense, is agreed to be a legitimate undertaking. But no such agreement exists about philosophy of history.[1]

It is perhaps worth asking how this situation has come about, since the enquiry may be expected to throw light on the subject-matter of the branch of study with which we propose to deal. Historical studies have flourished in Great Britain for two centuries and more; yet philosophy of history has been, until recent years, virtually non-existent. Why?

One reason is undoubtedly to be found in the general orientation of philosophical thought in Europe. Modern Western philosophy took its rise out of reflection on the extraordinary progress made

1. [This was written in 1949, and reference to the 'Note on books' at the end of this volume will show that much important work has been done on the subject since then. Even so, philosophy of history remains only marginally respectable in British universities.]

by mathematical physics in the late sixteenth and early seventeenth centuries, and its connection with natural science has remained unbroken ever since. The equation of knowledge proper with knowledge gained by the methods of science was made by almost every major philosopher from the time of Descartes and Bacon to that of Kant. It is true that amongst these thinkers two schools can be sharply distinguished: those who stressed the mathematical aspect of mathematical physics, and those who pointed to its basis in observation and dependence on experiment as being the most important thing about it. But though divided in this way, the writers in question were united in holding that, metaphysics and theology apart, physics and mathematics were the sole repositories of genuine knowledge. Nor is it surprising that the classical philosophers at least took this view, seeing that these sciences really were (again except for metaphysics and theology) the only developed branches of learning at the time when they wrote.

That British philosophers have hitherto had little to say about history can thus be partly explained by the general character of the modern European philosophical tradition. That tradition has always tended to look to the natural sciences for material for its studies, and has formed its criteria of what to accept as known by reference to scientific models. History, expelled from the body of knowledge proper by Descartes in part I of the *Discourse*, is still regarded with suspicion by his successors today. And in any case, history as we know it today, as a developed branch of learning with its own methods and standards, is a comparatively new thing: indeed, it scarcely existed before the nineteenth century. But these considerations, valid as they are, cannot explain the whole position. For in other European countries philosophy of history has become an accredited branch of study. In Germany and in Italy, at least, the problems of historical knowledge have excited, and continue to excite, a lively interest; but there is strangely little awareness of them in Great Britain. How can this difference of attitude be accounted for?

The answer, I think, is to be found by referring to some predominant characteristics of the British mind and temper. There are Germans who profess to believe that philosophical aptitude is not among the gifts possessed by inhabitants of these islands, because they have shown little liking for metaphysical speculation of the remoter kind. But to say this is to overlook the very distinguished contributions made by writers like Locke and Hume to *critical* philosophy, contributions which are at least as notable as those of the thinkers of any other country. It is in propounding and solving problems of philosophical analysis—problems which arise when we reflect on the nature and conditions of such activities as the attainment of knowledge in the sciences, or the doing of moral actions—that British thinkers have excelled. These problems have been well suited to the native genius, with its combination of caution and critical acumen. By contrast, metaphysics, understood as an attempt to devise some overall interpretation of experience or to explain all things in terms of a single all-embracing system, has found comparatively little favour here. Its distinguished proponents have been few, and in general it has been regarded with scepticism and distrust.

Once these facts are appreciated, the neglect of philosophy of history by British thinkers in the past becomes more intelligible. For philosophy of history, as traditionally conceived, was without doubt a metaphysical subject. We can see this by glancing briefly at its development.

The question who should get the credit for inventing philosophy of history is a disputed one: a case could be made out for giving it to the Italian philosopher Vico (1668–1744), though his work passed largely unnoticed in his own day, another for going much further back to the writings of St Augustine or even to some parts of the Old Testament. For practical purposes, however, we are justified in asserting that philosophy of history first attained recognition as a separate subject in the period which opened with the publication, in 1784, of the first part of Herder's *Ideas for a Philosophical History of Mankind* and closed soon after the appearance of Hegel's posthumous *Lectures on the Philosophy of History* in 1837. But the study as conceived in this period was very much a matter of metaphysical speculation. Its aim was to attain an understanding of the course of history as a whole; to show that, despite the many apparent anomalies and inconsequences it presented, history could be regarded as forming a unity embodying an overall plan, a plan which, if once we grasped it, would both illuminate the detailed course of events and enable us to view the historical process as, in a special sense, satisfactory to reason. And its exponents, in attempting to realise this aim, displayed the usual qualities of speculative metaphysicians: boldness of imagination, fertility of hypothesis, a zeal for unity which was not above doing violence to facts classified as 'merely' empirical. They professed to offer an insight into history more profound and valuable than anything which working historians could produce, an insight which, in the case of Hegel, by far the greatest of these writers, found its basis not in any direct study of historical evidence (though Hegel was not so cavalier about facts as he is sometimes made out to be), but in considerations which were purely philosophical. Philosophy of history, as practised by these writers, thus came to signify a speculative treatment of the whole course of history, a treatment in which it was hoped to lay bare the secret of history once and for all.

All this was anathema to the cautious British mind.[1] It savoured far too strongly of that philosophy of nature for which German metaphysicians of the period were already notorious. Philosophers of nature seemed, to unfriendly critics at least, to promise a short cut to the understanding of nature, a way of discovering facts without going through the tedious business of empirical enquiry. By their own admission their object was to achieve a 'speculative' treatment of natural processes; and speculation, in this context, was not easily distinguished from guesswork. In its worst examples their work was marked by a fantastic apriorism which discredited it utterly in the eyes of the sober. Philosophy of nature was thus regarded with deep distrust by British thinkers, who transferred their dislike of it to philosophy of history, which they took to be nothing more than an attempt to do in the sphere of history what philosophers of nature were attempting in their own province. In each case both project and results were thought to be absurd.

The bias thus engendered against philosophy of history has remained a permanent feature of British philosophy. It is most instructive in this connection to notice that the antipathy is by no means confined to a single school. It is not only empiricists who have neglected this branch of study. Towards the end of the nine-teenth and in the opening years of the twentieth century Continental philosophers of an idealist turn of mind (Dilthey and Rickert in

---

1. There were, of course, some to whom these ways of thinking were congenial, as the cases of Coleridge and Carlyle show. But in general Romanticism has made a poor showing in British philosophy.

Germany, Croce in Italy, may be mentioned as examples) seized on history as affording a form of knowledge which could be regarded as concrete and individual in comparison with the abstract, general knowledge offered by the natural sciences, and built their systems round that fact or supposed fact. But there was no corresponding movement in British idealism. It is true that Bradley began his career by writing a penetrating essay entitled 'The Presuppositions of Critical History'; but there is nothing to show that he attached any special importance to history in the working out of his general metaphysical view. His colleague Bosanquet certainly had no doubts about the matter. 'History,' he said, 'is a hybrid form of experience, incapable of any considerable degree of "being or trueness".'[1] A genuine idealism must be founded on the facts of aesthetic or religious experience, or again on those of social life; it was to these spheres, and not to history, that we must look for the concrete understanding of which Continental writers spoke. And Bosanquet's opinion was generally shared by all British idealists before Collingwood. Even today history remains an object of suspicion to some members of this school, if only because of the tendency shown by those who concern themselves with it to say that, as the only valid form of knowledge, it must absorb philosophy itself.[2]

§ 2. *Critical and speculative philosophy of history*

Such being the general reaction of British philosophers to the subject we are proposing to treat, the question may well be asked why we should presume to differ from them. If philosophy of history is thus generally despised, why venture to revive it? Now one answer to this might be that philosophy of history in its traditional form did not come to an end on the death of Hegel. It was continued, though in a very different guise, by Marx, and has been practised again in our own day by such writers as Spengler and Toynbee. Philosophy of history, in fact, like other parts of metaphysics, appears to exercise a continuous fascination on human

---

1. *The Principle of Individuality and Value*, pp. 78–9.
2. This tendency to what is called *historicism* (which has no essential connection with philosophy of history) is well illustrated by the later work of Collingwood, who was himself influenced in forming it by Croce and Gentile. For the attitude to it of a contemporary idealist the reader should consult the introduction by Professor T. M. Knox to Collingwood's posthumous book *The Idea of History*.

beings despite the repeated cry of its opponents that it consists of a set of nonsense statements. And a defence of a further enquiry into the traditional problems of the subject might well be developed along those lines. In the present context, however, I do not wish to ground myself on arguments which some readers at least are bound to find unconvincing. I want instead to try to show that there is a sense in which philosophers of every school should allow that philosophy of history is the name of a genuine enquiry.

As a preliminary to this I must point out the simple and familiar fact that the word 'history' is itself ambiguous. It covers (1) the totality of past human actions, and (2) the narrative or account we construct of them now. This ambiguity is important because it opens up at once two possible fields for philosophy of history. That study might be concerned, as it was in its traditional form briefly described above, with the actual course of historical events. It might, on the other hand, occupy itself with the processes of historical thinking, the means by which history in the second sense is arrived at. And clearly its content will be very different according to which of the two we choose.

To see the relevance of this distinction for our present purposes we have only to turn our attention for a moment to the parallel case of the natural sciences. Here there are in fact two terms for the enquiries corresponding to those we are distinguishing, though they are not always used with strict accuracy. They are philosophy of nature and philosophy of science. The first is concerned to study the actual course of natural events, with a view to the construction of a cosmology or account of nature as a whole. The second has as its business reflection on the process of scientific thinking, examination of the basic concepts used by scientists, and matters of that sort. In the terminology of Professor Broad, the first is a speculative, the second a critical discipline. And it needs very little reflection to see that a philosopher who rejects the possibility of the first of these studies is not thereby committed to rejecting the second.

It may be, as some philosophers would maintain, that philosophy of nature (in the sense of a study of the course of natural events in some way supplementary to that carried out by natural scientists) is an illegitimate undertaking; that cosmologies are, in fact, either summaries of scientific results (in which case they had best be left to scientists to construct) or idle fantasies of the imagination. But even if this is so, it does not follow that there is no such subject as philosophy of science. Even if the philosopher cannot add in any way to the sum of our knowledge of nature or to our understanding of natural processes, he may all the same have something useful to say about the character and presuppositions of scientific thinking, the proper analysis of scientific ideas and the relation of one branch of science to another, and his mastery of logical techniques may conceivably help to clear up practical difficulties in scientific work. He is scarcely likely to say anything of value on these subjects unless he has a fair acquaintance with the sort of things scientists do; but, all the same, the questions he is asking will not be scientific questions. They will belong not to the direct search for factual truth or understanding which is the object of scientific enquiry, but rather to the stage of reflection which ensues when we begin to consider the nature and implications of scientific activities themselves.

Now, as was said at the beginning, it would be generally agreed that philosophy of science is a perfectly genuine branch of study. Even the most anti-metaphysically minded philosopher would admit that. But in that case he ought also to admit the possibility of philosophy of history in one of its forms at least. For just as scientific thinking gives rise to two possible studies, one concerned with the activity itself, the other with its objects, so does historical thinking. 'Philosophy of history' is, in fact, the name of a double group of philosophical problems: it has both a speculative and an analytic part. And even those who reject the first of these may perfectly well (and indeed should) accept the second.

§ 3. *Critical philosophy of history*

What questions are, or ought to be, discussed by those who concern themselves with the two parts of our subject here distinguished? It seems to me that the problems of *critical* philosophy of history, if I may begin with that, fall into four main groups. It may help the reader if I try at this point to indicate briefly what these are.

(a) *History and other forms of knowledge.* The first group is made up of questions about the very nature of historical thinking. What sort of a thing is history and how does it relate to other studies? The point at issue here is the crucial one of whether historical knowledge is *sui generis*, or whether it can be shown to be identical in character

with some other form of knowledge—knowledge as pursued in the
natural sciences, for instance, or again perceptual knowledge.

The view of history perhaps most commonly accepted makes it
co-ordinate with perceptual knowledge. It holds that the essential
task of the historian is to discover individual facts about the past,
just as it is the essential task of perception to discover individual
facts about the present. And just as the data of perception constitute
the material on which the natural scientist works, so, it is argued,
the data of the historian provide material for the social scientist,
whose business it is to contribute to the all-important science of
man. But this neat division of labour, which assigns to the historian
the task of finding out what happened and to the social scientist
that of explaining it, breaks down when we turn to actual examples
of historical work. What immediately strikes us there is that historians are not content with the simple discovery of past facts: they
aspire, at least, not only to say what happened, but also to show
why it happened. History is not just a plain record of past events,
but what I shall call later a 'significant' record—an account in
which events are connected together. And the question immediately
arises what their being connected implies about the nature of
historical thinking.

Now one possible answer to this (it is sometimes taken as the
only possible answer) is that the historian connects his facts in
precisely the same way as the natural scientist connects his—by
seeing them as exemplifications of general laws. According to this
line of argument, historians have at their disposal a whole set of
generalisations of the form 'situations of A-type give rise to
situations of B-type', by means of which they hope to elucidate
their facts. It is this belief which lies behind the theory of the
nineteenth-century positivists that historical thinking is, in effect,
a form of scientific thinking. What these authors stressed was that
there are laws of history just as there are laws of nature; and they
argued that historians ought to concentrate on making these laws
explicit. But in actual fact historians have shown little or no interest
in this programme, preferring instead to give their attention, as
before, to the detailed course of individual events, yet claiming, all
the same, to offer some explanation of it. And their doing so
suggests the possibility at least that historical thinking is, after all,
a form of thinking of its own, coordinate with and not reducible

to scientific thinking. We cannot assume that it is on the strength
of one or two prima facie difficulties in the other theories mentioned:
the autonomy of history, if it is autonomous, clearly has to be
demonstrated on independent grounds. But that there is some case
for the view is hard to deny.

(*b*) *Truth and fact in history.* These questions about the status of
historical thinking and its relation to other studies ought, I believe,
to be regarded as genuine by philosophers of all schools. And the
same can be said of the second group of problems belonging to
critical philosophy of history, which centre round the conceptions
of truth and fact in history. Here, as in the problem of historical
objectivity which I shall discuss next, we have to do with questions
which arise in theory of knowledge generally, but have certain
special features when we consider them in relation to the sphere
of history.

These features are obvious enough when we ask what is an
historical fact, or again in virtue of what we can pronounce the
statements of historians to be true or false. We are apt to suppose
that the facts in any branch of learning must be in some way open
to direct inspection, and that the statements of experts in each
branch can be tested by their conformity with them. But whatever
the virtues of this theory elsewhere, it cannot be applied with
any plausibility to the field of history.

The most striking thing about history is that the facts it purports
to describe are past facts; and past facts are no longer accessible to
direct inspection. We cannot, in a word, test the accuracy of
historical statements by simply seeing whether they correspond
to a reality which is independently known. How then can we test
them? The answer which any practising historian would give to
this question would be that we do so by referring to historical
evidence. Although the past is not accessible to direct inspection
it has left ample traces of itself in the present, in the shape of documents, buildings, coins, institutions, procedures and so forth. And
it is upon these that any self-respecting historian builds his reconstruction of it: every assertion the historian makes, he would say,
must be supported by some sort of evidence, direct or indirect.
So-called historical statements which rest on any other basis (for
example, on the historian's unaided imagination) should be given

no credence. At their best they are inspired guesses; at their worst mere fiction.

This certainly gives us an intelligible working theory of historical truth, but not one which satisfies all philosophical scruples. We can see that if we reflect on the character of historical evidence itself. The traces of the past which are available in the present include, as I have already said, such things as documents, coins, procedures and so forth. But when we come to think about it, such things bear neither their meaning nor their authenticity on their face. Thus when an historian reads a statement in one or other of the 'original sources' for a period he is studying, he does not automatically accept it. His attitude to it, if he knows his job, is always critical: he has to *decide* whether or not to believe it, or again how much of it to believe. History proper, as Collingwood was never tired of pointing out, cannot be looked on as a scissors and paste affair: it is not made up by the historian's taking bits of wholly reliable information from either one or a whole series of 'authorities.' Historical facts have in every case to be established: they are never simply given. And this applies not merely to the finished products of the historian's thinking, but to the statements from which he starts as well; though, as we shall see later, this is not inconsistent with recognising that some of these statements are regarded by him as having a far higher degree of reliability than others.

We can sum this up by saying that it is the duty of the historian not only to base all his statements on the available evidence, but further to decide what evidence is available. Historical evidence, in other words, is not an ultimate datum to which we can refer to test the truth of historical judgments. But this, as will be obvious, reopens the whole question of fact and truth in history. With further attempts to deal with it—of which we may mention here the theory that *some* historical evidence (namely that provided by certain memory judgments) is, after all, irrefragable, and the opposing idealist contention that all history is contemporary history (i.e., that historical thinking is in reality concerned not with the past, but the present)—we cannot deal here. They will be the subject of discussion in a later chapter. But enough has perhaps been said to indicate that serious problems arise when we begin to reflect on these questions, and to make clear that they are a proper subject for philosophical enquiry.

(c) *Historical objectivity.* The third of our sets of questions concerns the notion of objectivity in history, a notion of which it is not too much to say that it cries out for critical scrutiny. The difficulties raised by this concept[1] can perhaps best be brought out by considering the two following not obviously compatible positions.

(i) On the one hand, every reputable historian acknowledges the need for some sort of objectivity and impartiality in his work: he distinguishes history from propaganda, and condemns those writers who allow their feelings and personal preconceptions to affect their reconstruction of the past as bad workmen who do not know their job. If the point were put to them, most historians could be got to agree that theirs was a primarily cognitive activity, concerned with an independent object, the past, whose nature they had to investigate for its own sake, though they would doubtless add that our knowledge of that object is always fragmentary and incomplete. Yet (ii) the fact remains that disagreements among historians are not only common but disturbingly stubborn, and that, once technical questions of precisely what conclusion can be drawn from this or that piece of evidence are regarded as settled, instead of an agreed interpretation of any period emerging, a plurality of different and apparently inconsistent readings of it is developed—Marxist and liberal, Catholic, Protestant and 'rationalist,' royalist and republican, and so on. These theories are held in such a way that their supporters think each of them to be, if not the final truth about the period under study, at any rate correct in essentials: a conviction which makes them repudiate all rival views as positively erroneous. And this can only suggest to a candid outside observer that the claim to scientific status often made for modern history at least is one which cannot be sustained, since historians have conspicuously failed to develop what may be called an historical 'consciousness in general,' a set of agreed canons of interpretation which all who work at the subject would be ready to acknowledge.

What are we to say about this situation? There seem to be three main ways in which we could try to deal with it.

First, we might attempt to maintain not only that historians are

1. Reference forward to pp. 36–7 may be found useful for the understanding of what follows.

influenced by subjective factors, but that they must be. Impartial history, so far from being an ideal, is a downright impossibility. In support of this we could point out that every historian looks at the past from a certain point of view, which he can no more avoid than he can jump out of his own skin. We could also maintain that the disagreements of historians, when carefully analysed, seem to turn on points which are not matter for argument, but depend rather on the interests and desires of the contending parties, whether in a personal or in a group capacity. Historical disputes, according to this way of thinking, are at bottom concerned not with what is true or false, but with what is and what is not desirable, and fundamental historical judgments are in consequence not strictly cognitive but 'emotive.' This would go far to abolish the distinction between history and propaganda, and therefore to undermine the claim that history is (or can become) a truly scientific study.

Secondly, we might try to argue that the past failure of historians to reach objective truth is no evidence that it will always elude them, and attempt to show that the development of a common historical consciousness is not out of the question. In so doing we should be adopting the position of the nineteenth-century positivists from which the German philosopher Dilthey started (though Dilthey changed his mind about it later): that objective history ought to rest on an objective study of human nature. The difficulties of this project are clearly enormous, and the positivist view of it at least is altogether too simple; but it should not be rejected for that reason alone. It is clearly a point in its favour that, as we shall argue later, general judgments about human nature have an important part to play in historical interpretation and explanation.

Lastly, we could maintain that the concept of historical objectivity is radically different from that of scientific objectivity, the difference coming out in the fact that whilst all reputable historians condemn biased and tendentious work, they do not so clearly endorse the scientific ideal of wholly impersonal thinking. The work of the historian, like that of the artist, may be thought to be in some sense an expression of his personality, and it is plausible to argue that this is of vital account for the subject we are considering. For though it is fashionable to dismiss art as a wholly practical activity, the fact remains that we do often speak as if it were in some sense cognitive too. The artist, we say, is not content only to have and express his emotions: he wants also to communicate what he takes to be a certain vision or insight into the nature of things, and would claim truth and objectivity for his work for that very reason. And it might be maintained that the best way of dealing with the problem of historical objectivity is to assimilate historical thinking in this respect to the thinking of the artist. History might then be said to give us a series of different but not incompatible portraits of the past, each reflecting it from a different point of view.

There are obvious difficulties in this as in the two preceding theories, but they cannot be discussed here. The most I can hope to have achieved in this short survey is to have shown that my original statement that the concept of objectivity in history cries out for critical scrutiny is only too patently true, and to have directed the reader's attention to some lines of thinking about it. With this I must leave the matter for the present, and pass on to the fourth and last of my groups of problems in critical philosophy of history.

(*d*) *Explanation in history.* The central problem in this group is that of the nature of historical explanation. The question here is whether there are any peculiarities about the way the historian explains (or attempts to explain) the events he studies. We have seen already that there is a case for saying that history is, typically, narrative of past actions arranged in such a way that we see not only what happened but also why. We must now ask what sort, or sorts, of 'why' are involved in history.

We can best approach this question by considering the way in which the concept of explanation is used in the natural sciences. It is a philosophical commonplace that scientists no longer attempt to explain the phenomena with which they deal in any ultimate sense: they do not propose to tell us why things are what they are to the extent of revealing the purpose behind nature. They are content with the far more modest task of building up a system of observed uniformities in terms of which they hope to elucidate any situation which falls to be examined. Given any such situation, their procedure is to show that it exemplifies one or more general laws, which can themselves be seen to follow from, or connect with, other laws of a wider character. The main features of this process are, first, that it consists in the resolution of particular events into cases of general laws, and secondly that it involves nothing more than an external view of the phenomena under consideration (since the scientist is not professing to reveal the purpose behind them). It can thus be said to result in an understanding which is properly described as 'abstract.' Now it has been claimed by many writers on philosophy of history that historical understanding is not thus abstract but is, in some sense, concrete. It is clear enough that the question whether there is anything in this contention depends on whether historians explain their facts in the same way as natural scientists explain theirs, or whether they can be shown to possess some peculiar insight into their subject-matter enabling them to grasp its individual nature.

There are some philosophers who have only to pose such a question to answer it in the negative. Explanation, they hold, is and can be of only one type, the type employed in scientific thinking. A process of explanation is essentially a process of deduction, and at the centre of it there is thus always something expressible in general terms. But to conclude on such grounds that there can be no special concept of explanation in history is the reverse of convincing. The right way of tackling the question, one would have supposed, would be to begin by examining the steps historians actually take when they set out to elucidate an historical event or set of events. And when we do that we are immediately struck by the fact that they do not seem to employ generalisations in the same way as scientists do. Ostensibly at least, historians do not attempt to illuminate particular situations by referring to other situations of the same type; their initial procedure at any rate is quite different. Thus when asked to explain a particular event— say, the British general strike in 1926—they will begin by tracing connections between that event and others with which it stands in inner relationship (in the case in question, certain previous events in the history of industrial relations in Great Britain). The under-lying assumption here is that different historical events can be regarded as going together to constitute a single process, a whole of which they are all parts and in which they belong together in a specially intimate way. And the first aim of the historian, when he is asked to explain some event or other, is to see it as part of such a process, to locate it in its context by mentioning other events with which it is bound up.

Now this process of 'colligation,' as we may call it (following the usage of the nineteenth-century logician Whewell), is certainly a peculiarity of historical thinking, and is consequently of great importance when we are studying the nature of historical explanation. But we should not try to make too much of it. Some writers on the subject seem to leap from the proposition that we can establish inner connections between certain historical events to the far more general assertion that history is wholly intelligible, and argue in consequence that it is therefore superior to the natural sciences. This is clearly a mistake. The truth would seem to be that though historical thinking does thus possess certain peculiarities of its own, it is not *toto caelo* different from scientific thinking. In particular, it is hard to deny that the historian, like the scientist, does make appeal to general propositions in the course of his study, though he does not make these explicit in the same way as the scientist does. History differs from the natural sciences in that it is not the aim of the historian to formulate a system of general laws; but this does not mean that no such laws are presupposed in historical thinking. In fact, as I hope to show in detail later, the historian does make constant use of generalisations, in particular generalisations about the different ways in which human beings react to different kinds of situation. History thus presupposes general propositions about human nature, and no account of historical thinking would be complete without proper appreciation of that fact.

So much by way of preliminary description of what seem to be the leading problems of critical philosophy of history. Our survey should have made clear both that there are a number of genuine difficulties in the subject, and that they are the sort of difficulty with which analytic philosophers traditionally deal (though they have not been considered at all carefully by philosophers in Great Britain until recently). The main trouble about them is perhaps that they seem to be particularly closely interrelated, so that in treating of one group—say, that which concerns historical objectivity—we find ourselves forced to raise questions which strictly belong to another—questions about the relations between history and the sciences, for example, or again about historical explanation. But this difficulty, if acute in philosophy of history, is by no means confined to that subject; and we must do what we can to deal with it, remembering that our grouping of problems is not to be thought of as possessing any inherent value in itself, but is merely a methodological device designed to prevent our asking too many questions at once.

§ 4. *Speculative philosophy of history*

To turn now to the problems which belong to philosophy of history in its speculative or metaphysical part, we must admit from the first that there is much more disagreement about whether these are genuine problems or not. Some philosophers would say that the only topics with which philosophy of history should concern itself are analytic problems of the kind already described, and that all further enquiries (such as those pursued by writers like Hegel) are in fact futile. But it must be confessed that there is at any rate a strong tendency to raise questions about the course of history as well as about the nature of historical thinking.

We may distinguish two groups of such questions. The first includes all those metaphysical problems which, as has already been made clear, were dealt with in what I am calling traditional philosophy of history. The fundamental point with which these philosophers were concerned can be put if we say that they sought to discover the meaning and purpose of the whole historical process. History as presented by ordinary historians seemed to them to consist of little more than a succession of disconnected events, utterly without rhyme or reason. There was no attempt in 'empirical' history, as it was called, to go beyond actual happenings to the plan which lay behind them, no attempt to reveal the underlying plot of history. That there was such a plot they thought obvious, if history was not to be regarded as wholly irrational; and accordingly they set themselves to find it. The task of philosophy of history, they thought, was to write such an account of the detailed course of historical events that its 'true' significance and 'essential' rationality were brought out. As we have seen already, it is easy enough to criticise such a project; and in fact the programme was condemned both by working historians (who saw in it an attempt to take away their jobs) and by anti-metaphysical philosophers (who thought it wholly incapable of realisation). But the fundamental problem it raises—the problem, to call it by a crude name, of the meaning of history—is one which clearly has a recurrent interest, and no survey of our present subject could neglect it altogether.

The second group of questions is perhaps not strictly philosophical at all, though, thanks to the vogue of Marxism, it is with it that the general public most commonly takes philosophy of history to be concerned. The Marxist philosophy of history, so-called, has more aspects than one: in so far as it attempts to show that the course of history is tending to the creation of a classless communist society, for example, it comes near to being a philosophy of history of the traditional kind. But its main purpose is to put forward a theory of historical interpretation and causation. If Marx is right, the main moving factors in history are all economic; and no interpretation of the detailed course of events which fails to recognise this has any value. Now it must be said from the first thates the question what are the main moving factors in history do not appear to be philosophical. It is a question which can be answered only by a study of actual causal connections in history; and why a philosopher should be thought specially equipped to make such a study is not apparent. It could obviously be undertaken with far more profit by an intelligent working historian. Moreover, it should result in the formulation not of a self-evident truth, but of an empirical hypothesis, to be tested by its efficacy in throwing light on individual historical situations. In so far as this is true, the working out of a theory of historical interpretation seems to belong to history itself rather than to philosophy of history, just as the determination of what causal factors are of most importance in the material world belongs to the sciences and not to philosophy of science.

There is, however, some excuse for regarding Marx's own views on these matters as having more than a touch of the philosophical about them. We can say that the Marxist theory of historical interpretation is philosophical in so far as it presents its main contention not as a mere empirical hypothesis, but as something much more like an *a priori* truth. Marx, as we find if we look at his views carefully, does not appear to be claiming only that economic factors are *as a matter of fact* the most potent forces determining the course of history; he seems to be holding further that, things being what they are, such factors are *and must be* the basic elements in every historical situation. We have only to reflect on the way in which Marxists use their thesis to see that they assign it a greater validity than would be warranted if they did regard it as an empirical hypothesis. What, in fact, they appear to be doing is advocating the principle of historical materialism as a necessary truth, such that no future experience could possibly confute it. And if this is really correct their procedure certainly deserves the attention of philosophers.

The implications of these remarks should not be misunderstood. I am not suggesting that the attempt, by Marxists and others, to propound general theories of historical interpretation is in any way improper. I should have thought on the contrary that it is something in which all concerned with the study of history must be interested. My point about it is that the task of working out such a theory belongs not to the philosopher but to the historian. Marx's contribution to the understanding of history, in fact, was not made to philosophy of history in the proper sense at all. But the Marxist theory is of interest to the philosopher because of the kind of importance Marx appears to attach to his main principle. The unrestricted validity assigned by Marxists to this principle is inconsistent with its being regarded as a mere empirical hypothesis (though not with its having been *suggested* by experience); and the question what justification there is for regarding it in that way certainly deserves close attention.

All these points will be discussed in detail at a later stage. The purpose of the present exposition is only to illustrate the kind of question with which philosophy of history deals or might be thought to deal. We may summarise by saying that if the philosopher can be said to have any specific concern with the course of history, it must be with that course as a whole, i.e., with the significance of the whole historical process. This second part of our study, in fact, must be either metaphysical or non-existent.[1] And doubtless to say that will create a prejudice against it in some readers. But it is not clear that such a prejudice is justified, either

1. This might be denied on the ground that it is part of the function of philosophy of history to elucidate such concepts as 'progress', 'historical event', 'historical period'. I am not sure myself that it is, but if it is, the matter obviously connects closely with the topics mentioned in § 3 above.

in general or in the specific case before us. To assume that it is
without discussion would scarcely be justifiable.

§ 5. *Plan of the book*

The treatment of philosophy of history in the present volume will
fall into two parts corresponding to those just distinguished. In
the first and longer of these we shall be occupied primarily with the
nature of historical thinking. We shall state, or attempt to state,
the most prominent features of that sort of thinking, trying to
discover those among them which mark it off from thinking of
other kinds. We shall discuss its presuppositions and examine the
epistemological character of its products. Our procedure here will
be purely reflective: starting from the fact that people do think
about historical questions, our aim will be to discover what precisely
they are doing. By these means we shall be able to touch on all
those questions which were said above to belong to critical philosophy of history. It is scarcely necessary to emphasise that, in an
elementary work like this, it will not be possible to do more than
indicate what are the main problems which arise and to discuss,
more or less dogmatically, one or two of the most obvious solutions
of them. But even that may have its uses in so neglected a subject
as this.

The second part of our enquiry, concerned with the traditional
problems of philosophy of history, will necessarily be even more
sketchy. The most we shall be able to do here, in fact, is to examine
in outline one or two celebrated attempts to construct philosophies
of history of the metaphysical kind, and to draw from reflection
on them some conclusions about the feasibility of the whole enterprise. By way of appendix to this part I propose to undertake a
brief consideration of historical materialism, developing the points
made about it in the present chapter. If any reader is dissatisfied
with the brevity of this treatment I can only say I am sorry; but I
must make it plain that, in my view, a final decision about the
validity of the theory in question rests not with the philosopher
but with the historian himself.

2

HISTORY AND THE SCIENCES

§ 1. *Preliminary characterisation of history.*
History and sense-perception

In the preceding chapter we have assumed that there is a distinctive sort of thinking called historical thinking, and have pointed out some of the prima facie problems it seems to raise. We must now subject our assumption to examination, and attempt to say more precisely what sort of a thing historical thinking is and how it differs from other sorts of thinking—thinking in the natural sciences, for example. We shall thus be opening up the whole problem of the status of historical knowledge, and touching on the difficult issues raised by the enquiry whether, and in what sense, history can claim to be a scientific study.

Probably the best way of approaching the question is to ask what it is the historian is seeking to investigate and what he hopes to discover. The first answer that occurs is the obvious one that he aims at an intelligent reconstruction of the past. And it might be thought that that in itself would serve to mark off history as a separate branch of knowledge. The natural sciences, it is easy to suppose, are concerned with the world around us; they rely on sense-perception for their data. History, by way of contrast, is concerned with the past, and memory-impressions must hence form an indispensable part of its raw-material. But, in fact, the contrast between history and the natural sciences is not so sharp as that. In the first place, it is not true that the scientist is concerned with the present to the exclusion of the past. Quite apart from the fact that memory-knowledge enters into all present perceptual judgments about objects, it is only necessary to remember the existence of such studies as geology and palaeontology to see that there are branches of scientific enquiry which study the past rather than the present. And again, it cannot be held that history is, without qualification, a study of the past. There are large portions of the past of which history as normally understood takes no cognisance whatever—for instance, all those ages which preceded the evolution of man to something like the sort of creature he is now.

To define history as *the* study of the past, and attempt to ground its autonomy as a form of knowledge on that point, can thus not be defended. But, of course, history is, in some sense, *a* study of the past. What past? The answer is the past of human beings. History begins to be interested in the past when human beings first appear in it. Its essential concern is with human experiences and actions. It is true, of course, that history records not merely what human beings did and suffered, but also a considerable number of *natural* events in the past—earthquakes, floods, droughts and the like. But its interest in these events is strictly subsidiary. The historian is not concerned, at any point of his work, with nature for its own sake; only with nature as a background to human activities. If he mentions natural events, it is because those events had effects on the lives of the men and women whose experiences he is describing. Had they had no such effects, he would not have mentioned them.

That this is not mere dogmatism the reader can see for himself by reflecting on actual historical writings. A history of the world does not normally begin with speculations about the origins of the universe, nor does it include an account of the mutations of plant and animal species once life had appeared on this planet. Its effective range is very much shorter: it concentrates on the activities of man as known over a comparatively brief space of time. And in case anyone thinks that this is mere short-sightedness on the part of historians, reflecting the anti-scientific bent of their education, and points out that H. G. Wells in his *Outline of History* offered something much more comprehensive, it may be relevant here to mention that even Wells was primarily concerned in his work with the activities of human beings, and that his early chapters, whatever their ostensible purpose, were, in fact, inserted because he thought they threw light on human nature. What stress to lay on the natural background to men's actions, and how far to connect those actions with man's animal nature, are points which individual historians must decide for themselves. Wells chose to go a long way back, but did not change the nature of history in doing so.

Let us therefore take it as agreed that it is the human past which is the primary object of the historian's study. The next point for consideration is the type of understanding he aims at.

Here we have two possibilities to consider. The first is that the historian confines himself (or should confine himself) to an exact description of what happened, constructing what may be called a plain narrative of past events. The other is that he goes beyond such a plain narrative and aims not merely at saying what happened but also at (in some sense) explaining it. In the second case the kind of narrative he constructs may be described as 'significant' rather than 'plain.'

The relevance of the distinction here suggested can be brought out by considering a parallel problem. A study of the weather for a given district over a given period might obviously be undertaken at two levels, which we may here distinguish, somewhat invidiously, as amateur and professional. At the first of these the observer would restrict himself to a full and accurate record of details of barometric pressures, temperatures, wind directions and forces, rainfall, etc., thus producing a simple chronicle of the weather of the district. At the second he would not be content with such a chronicle, but would strive not only to record but also, so far as his data enabled him, to understand the events with which he was dealing, by tracing the working in them of the general laws which meteorology establishes.

The question whether the historian constructs a plain or what I am calling a significant narrative of past events is the question whether his procedure approximates to that of the amateur or to that of the professional meteorologist in my illustration. But the problem should not be misunderstood. The point at issue is not that of the ultimate identity of historical with scientific thinking: that is a question which arises only at a later stage. It is rather that of whether the level at which history moves is comparable to the level of simple perception or to that of science. If the first is the true account, we may say that the proper task of the historian is to tell us, in the famous phrase of Ranke, 'precisely what happened', and leave the matter at that; if the second, we must agree that the sort of narrative the historian has to construct is a 'significant' narrative, leaving the question how it can be such (i.e., in what its significance consists) to subsequent investigation.

Now I think it is not difficult to show that history proper does involve significant rather than plain narrative of the past experience of human beings. The historian is not content to tell us merely what happened; he wishes to make us see why it happened, too. In other words, he aims, as was implied at the beginning, at a reconstruction of the past which is both intelligent and intelligible. It is true that historians often fail to reach this high level: they lack either the evidence or the insight required for an adequate reconstruction, and find themselves in consequence driven to recite isolated facts without being able to fit them into a coherent picture. But their doing so testifies only to the general difficulties under which historians work, not to any inherent weakness in the historical ideal. The truth is that history is a much more difficult subject than it is often taken to be, and that its successful pursuit demands the fulfilment of many conditions, not all of which are in the power of historians themselves. But that historical truth is hard to achieve is no reason for denying its special nature.

There is a distinction made by Croce, at the beginning of his book on the *Theory and History of Historiography*, which may be found illuminating in this connection. Croce there contrasts history proper with chronicle, describing the first as the living thought of the past, whilst the second is, as it stands, dead and unintelligible. Croce's own exploitation of this distinction in the interest of his theory that all history is contemporary history need not here concern us. But we should, I think, recognise that his distinction does answer to a real difference in levels of historical understanding. The sort of knowledge we have of the history of ancient Greek painting, to take an example of Croce's own, is very different from that which we have of e.g. the political history of nineteenth-century Europe; and indeed the difference is so profound that they may almost be said to belong to separate genres. It is not only that in the case of nineteenth-century political history we have far more material to work on than when we are dealing

B

with the history of Greek painting, of which very little direct evidence remains. There is also the fact that, because we stand nearer to the nineteenth century, we can enter far more easily into the thoughts and feelings of the age, and so use our evidence in a far more effective way. The narrative we can construct of nine-teenth-century political history is both full and coherent: events in it can be presented in such a manner that their development seems to be orderly and intelligible. A history of this sort is close-knit and consequential. But a history of Greek painting, or what passes for such a history, is a sorry affair by comparison, consisting of little but the names and approximate dates of a few celebrities, with the titles of their works as recorded by ancient authors. It gives us no insight into the actual development of painting in the ancient world, but is really only an unsatisfactory chronicle, a mere skeleton of a history.

The point on which I want to insist is that, though it is possible to find these two levels of chronicle and history proper throughout written history—though it is possible to find elements of chronicle in the most sophisticated history, and of history proper in the most primitive chronicle—the historical ideal is always to get away from the stage of chronicle and attain that of history itself. What every historian seeks for is not a bare recital of unconnected facts, but a smooth narrative in which every event falls as it were into its natural place and belongs to an intelligible whole. In this respect the ideal of the historian is in principle identical with that of the novelist or the dramatist. Just as a good novel or a good play appears to consist not in a series of isolated episodes, but in the orderly development of the complex situation from which it starts, so a good history possesses a certain unity of plot or theme. And where we fail to find such a unity we experience a feeling of dissatisfaction: we believe we have not understood the facts we set out to investigate as well as we should.

Now if this is at all right (and the reader should be warned that it is put forward not as a final analysis, but merely as a prima facie description of the actual procedure and aspirations of historians), I think we can conclude with assurance that any attempt to regard history as simply coordinate with sense-perception must be mis-taken. If we are asked whether the thinking of the historian moves on the perceptual or the scientific level, these alternatives being taken as exhaustive, there is only one answer we can give. But to give that answer is not to solve the problem of the status of historical thinking. For it raises at once the question of the sense, if any, in which it is proper to *identify* historical and scientific thinking, to say, in the well-known words of J. B. Bury, that 'history is a science, no less and no more.' To this question we must now turn our attention.

§ 2. *Features of scientific knowledge*

What do we mean by calling a body of knowledge a science? We mean, in the first place, to distinguish it from a collection of random bits of information. All the facts I learned yesterday may, for certain imaginable purposes, need to be considered together; but nobody would regard them as constituting a science. The different propositions of a science, in contrast to the constituents of such an aggregate, are systematically related. A science, whatever else it is, is a body of knowledge acquired as the result of an attempt to study a certain subject-matter in a methodical way, following a determinate set of guiding principles. And it is the fact that we approach our material with such a set of principles in mind which gives unity and system to our results. The fundamental point here is that we are asking questions from a definite set of presuppositions, and our answers are connected just because of that. It should be added that the truth of this contention is not affected by the fact that scientific enquirers are often unaware of their own presuppositions: we need not have a principle explicitly in mind to be capable of using it in our thinking.

A science is thus to be understood at least as a body of systematically related knowledge, arranged in an orderly way. But is that sufficient to provide a definition? It has been pointed out[1] that it is not, for if it were we should have to agree that a railway time-table or a telephone directory were examples of scientific textbooks. The information in such works is arrived at by methodical enquiries and arranged in an orderly manner, but it would not normally be said to be scientific information. What makes us refuse it the title? The answer is that we tend to employ the word 'scientific' only where we have to do with a body of *general* propositions. A science, we should say, is a collection not of particular but of

1. cf. Cohen and Nagel's *Introduction to Logic and Scientific Method,* p.81 of the abridged edition.

universal truths, expressible in sentences which begin with such words as 'whenever,' 'if ever,' 'any' and 'no.' It is a commonplace to say that scientists are not interested in particulars for their own sake, only in particulars as being of a certain kind, as instances of general principles. That account of scientific knowledge was given by Aristotle, and it is repeated in textbooks on scientific method to this day.

This point about the general character of the propositions we call scientific is closely connected with another. We tend to think of scientific knowledge as knowledge which is always in some degree useful, useful in that it enables us to control the present or to predict the future. This statement should not be misunderstood. The point is not that we should refuse the name of science to a study whose utility could not be immediately seen: there are plenty of branches of science which seem on the face of things to be pursued for their own sake, without regard to any practical results we may expect from them. It is rather that, where we have scientific knowledge, we suppose always that it *might* be turned to practical account, in the way in which the abstract results of geology, for example, are turned to practical account in mining operations or those of mechanics in bridge-building. And the feature of scientific truths which makes this result possible is just their general character, which enables them to be used for purposes of prediction. Because the scientist is interested in the events he studies not as individual events, but as cases of a certain type, his knowledge carries him beyond the limits of his immediate experience and enables him to anticipate, and so perhaps to control, future happenings. It is because science generalises and so gives rise to predictions that it can render us, in Descartes' striking phrase, 'masters and possessors of nature.'

There is one last feature of scientific thinking as commonly understood which deserves a mention before we pass on to ask how all this bears on the status of history. I refer to the fact that the truth or falsity of scientific hypotheses is generally thought to be independent of the personal circumstances or private views of the persons who established them. Scientific statements, on this interpretation, lay claim to universal acceptance; they are not a proper field for the display of partisanship of any kind. To say this is not, of course, to commit ourselves to the absurd doctrine that there can be no arguing about scientific results: there can and must be controversies inside any science, and even accepted results must be open to correction as fresh evidence is forthcoming or new ways of interpreting old evidence are thought out. But all this is possible without the scientist's giving up his fundamental principle, that the conclusions he comes to are arrived at on grounds which other observers can scrutinise and share. Scientific theories and arguments may be difficult for the layman to understand; but if they are to deserve their name, they must never be esoteric in the bad sense of holding only on the strength of some alleged personal insight or for a group of specially privileged persons. It is by this test that we reject the scientific pretensions of astrology and have doubts about the completely scientific character of at least some of the studies grouped together under the title of psychical research.

We may sum up the results of this brief attempt to bring out the main features of the common conception of science and scientific knowledge as follows. We apply the term 'science' to knowledge which (a) is methodically arrived at and systematically related; (b) consists of, or at least includes, a body of general truths; (c) enables us to make successful predictions and so to control the future course of events, in some measure at least; (d) is objective, in the sense that it is such as every unprejudiced observer ought to accept if the evidence were put before him, whatever his personal predilections or private circumstances.

§ 3. *History and scientific knowledge*

With these considerations in mind, let us now attempt to determine the question whether history is a science.

That history is a scientific study in the sense of one pursued according to a method and a technique of its own is not likely to be denied. The conclusions which historians seek to establish are arrived at by the examination of a clearly defined subject-matter— the actions and sufferings of human beings in the past—carried out according to rules which successive generations of enquirers have rendered increasingly precise. On this matter there is hardly room for serious controversy. We have only to reflect on the fact that there is a class of professional historians, whose ability to deal with the material they study is entirely different from that of the ordinary man. Teaching advanced history, as anyone who has

experience of the subject knows, is not so much a matter of communicating facts as of imparting a certain technique for establishing
and interpreting them. And this technique, as we have already
remarked, has been substantially improved in the course of time,
in the last two centuries in particular, so that mistakes which highly
skilled writers made in the past can now be avoided by scholars of
only average competence.

It will be objected here that this is to exaggerate the difficulties
of historical understanding. Surely, it will be said, the point which
we find most striking in comparing the productions of historians
with those of natural scientists is that the former are intelligible to
persons with no professional training, whilst the latter are full of
technicalities which cannot be understood except by the expert.
But from the fact that history is written in everyday language,
having developed no special vocabulary of its own, it does not
follow that any fool can write it. The truth is that there is all the
difference in the world, in this as in other branches of learning,
between an amateur and a professional approach, though the
distinction is less obvious in history than it is elsewhere. This is
explained by the fact that we are all forced by the exigencies of
everyday life to make some use of the techniques of the historian.
We cannot read our daily papers intelligently without asking
questions about the reliability of the information they contain: the
evaluating of testimony, among the most important of the historian's
tasks, is something we must all undertake. That is clear enough, but
it is equally clear that we cannot all carry out the undertaking with
equal skill, and that a person with a training in historical method
has in this matter an enormous advantage over one who has only
his untrained intelligence on which to rely. Anyone who doubts
that and thinks that history is an affair of common sense and
nothing else may be invited to put his opinion to a practical test:
to take, say, a collection of documents dealing with the origins of
the first world war and construct on that basis a history of the
events which led to it. He will be surprised at the difficulties into
which he will fall and shocked at the simplicities in his thinking
which any professional historian will point out.

I propose therefore to take it that history can be described as
scientific in one respect at any rate, namely that it is a study with
its own recognised methods, which must be mastered by anyone

who hopes to be proficient at it. The question now arises how it stands in regard to the other three characteristics noted above.

So far as the second of our points is concerned, there seems to be a clear difference between history and the sciences; for the most casual acquaintance with historical work is enough to establish that it does not issue in a series of explicit generalisations. It is true that history is sometimes said to point to certain 'lessons,' and these certainly take the form of general truths: Lord Acton's celebrated dictum that 'all power corrupts, and absolute power corrupts absolutely' is an example. But though judgments of that sort are found from time to time in historical works, it cannot be said that they constitute the historian's main concern.

The central preoccupation of the historian, there seems no doubt, is not with generalities, but with the precise course of individual events: it is this which he hopes to recount and render intelligible. He wants, as we said before, to say precisely what happened and, in doing so, to explain why it happened as it did. And this means that his attention must be concentrated on the events which are the immediate object of his scrutiny: unlike the scientist, he is not all the time led beyond those events to consideration of the general principles which they illustrate. He is interested, for example, in the French Revolution of 1789 or the English Revolution of 1688 or the Russian Revolution of 1917; not (except incidentally) in the general character of revolutions as such. That is why the average history book ends when the writer has finished his account of the period under review; if the historian's interests were the same as the scientist's it would include another chapter, the most important in the work, in which the main lessons of the events in question would be set out in general terms.

A sceptical reader may remain unconvinced of the soundness of the argument here for two reasons. One is the existence in historical works of explicit generalisations of the kind exemplified by Lord Acton's dictum; to these I shall return. The other, which can be dealt with more easily, is the consideration that historical thinking does involve a certain element of generality which the above account appears to exclude.

I refer here to the fact that historians are not content to recount the events of a given period seriatim; they further conceive it to be their business to elucidate, for example, the temper and characteristics

of a whole age or people. Thus they write on such topics as
medieval England or the Enlightenment in France or the age of
the Victorians, and contrive to tell us in the course of their works
a good deal about the *general* characteristics of men who lived in
those times and places. But though this activity of theirs is very
important, and certainly falls within their proper province, it
affords in itself no ground for confusing historical with scientific
thinking. For the judgments to which it gives rise, though general
in comparison with statements of individual facts, are not universal
judgments in the true sense; they are simply highly condensed
summaries of particular occurrences.

A brief comparison of historical with scientific procedure proper
will bring this out. When a physicist formulates laws about the
behaviour of moving bodies, those laws are intended by him to
apply to anything which satisfies, has satisfied or will satisfy the
definition of that term; in the language of logic, such laws refer to
'open' classes, classes whose members can never be enumerated
because they are potentially infinite in number. But when historians
discuss the outlook of, say, educated men in eighteenth-century
France, they are referring to a class which is 'closed', one whose
members could in principle be enumerated. They are talking not,
as a scientist (e.g. a sociologist) would, about all men, past, present
and future, who have certain characteristics, but about all *the* men
who in fact lived at a certain time and in a certain area. And these
are two very different things.

I do not wish to disguise the fact that this subject of generalisation in history is a tricky one, on which a good deal more will need
to be said; but the reader may be willing to grant at this point that
there is at least a prima facie case for differentiating history from
natural science in regard to it. And the impression will perhaps
be confirmed if we pass on to consider the question of prediction
in history. As we saw above, the scientist's ability to make successful
predictions springs directly from his preoccupation with what is
typical, or of general interest, in the events he investigates. Conversely, the fact that, on the surface at least, historians are not concerned to predict at all would argue that their fundamental attitude
to the facts is quite different from that which scientists take up.

That historians study the past for its own sake, not for any light
the study may be expected to throw on the future course of events,

would be generally accounted a platitude. But the matter is perhaps not quite so simple as this suggests. In the first place, we have to ask whether the historian's concern with the past is as disinterested as at first sight appears. Surely it is not absurd to maintain that we study the past because we think the study will illuminate the present, and should not do so if we had no such belief. If the past were utterly irrelevant to the present, should we take any interest in it at all? And if it is pointed out that this can be admitted without turning historians into prophets (for the present is after all not the future), we may counter by asking whether it is not the case that study of the history of a country or a movement does put us in a better position to forecast its future. A person who knows a good deal about, say, the history of Germany is in some respects at least better equipped to say how Germany is likely to develop in the future than one who is utterly ignorant of that history. Historians may not be prophets, but they are often in a position to prophesy.

There is a further point to be considered in this connection. It has been said that whilst it is certainly not the business of historians to predict the future, it is very much their business to 'retrodict'[1] the past: to establish, on the basis of present evidence, what the past must have been like. And it is argued that the procedure of the historian in 'retrodicting' is exactly parallel to that of the scientist in predicting, since in each case the argument proceeds from the conjunction of particular premises (that so-and-so is the case now) with general truths, in the case of science laws of nature, in that of history laws governing human behaviour in situations of this kind or that.

These considerations reopen the whole question of the place of generalisations in historical thinking, but we shall not pursue the questions they raise further in the present context. We must be content to reaffirm the surface difference between history and science in regard to the second and third of our points. Scientists, as we saw, are primarily interested in general truths, and they do make it their business to predict; historians, by way of contrast, are primarily occupied with individual events, and seldom give expression to truly universal conclusions in the course of their work. This concentration of theirs on what individually happened

1. This useful term was suggested, I believe, by Prof. G. Ryle. [In a review of the first edition of this book Prof. H. B. Acton pointed out that 'retrodiction' was used by J. M. Robertson as early as 1895.]

perhaps explains their failure to predict, despite the advantage
which their work gives them in this matter over those who have no
historical knowledge. But we must leave this subject, and that of
'retrodiction', for further discussion later.

The problems raised for history by the fourth characteristic of
scientific thinking—its objectivity—are so complex that they
demand a chapter to themselves. For the present I must be content
to refer the reader back to the brief discussion in Chapter 1, from
which he will gather that there is a sense in which history does
claim to be an objective study, if only because historical statements
and interpretations are intended by their authors to be true or false.
But the subject is grossly misrepresented if we attempt to state a
conclusion about it in a simple formula, and it will be well to reserve
judgment until full discussion is possible. Fortunately we can do
this without prejudice to the determination of our main point in
the present chapter.

§ 4. *Two theories of historical thinking*

Let us now attempt to sum up the position as it stands at the
present stage of the argument. After rejecting the suggestion that
history is coordinate with sense-perception (that it is simply a
backward extension of present experience), we passed on to consider
its relations to the sciences. We enumerated various characteristics
of scientific thinking, and asked if anything corresponding to them
could be found in history. And our result has been a somewhat
indecisive one, for though we found history to possess one of the
characteristics mentioned, it was less easy to be sure about the
others. It was, however, evident that the whole orientation of the
historian's thought is different from that of the scientist, in that the
historian is primarily concerned with what individually happened
in the past, whilst the scientist's aim is to formulate universal laws.
And this difference will remain even if it should turn out that
general truths are presupposed in historical thinking, without
being made explicit there. At least no historian has as his main
object to arrive at truths of that kind.[1]

What is the moral of this situation? Philosophers have, in fact,
drawn two quite different conclusions from it and produced two

1. Prof. Toynbee may seem an exception to this dictum. For a brief discussion
of his views see Chapter 8 below.

quite different theories of historical thinking to meet the various points made above. I shall end this chapter with a sketch of these rival theories and a brief discussion of some points of strength and weakness in each.

The first theory, which originated in Germany towards the end of the last century, was taken up a little later by the Italian philosopher Croce and passed into English philosophy through his follower, R. G. Collingwood, is the standard idealist account of historical knowledge.[1] Roughly it runs as follows. History, because it offers a connected body of knowledge methodically arrived at, is a science; but it is a science of a peculiar kind. It is not an abstract but a concrete science, and it terminates not in general knowledge but in knowledge of individual truths. That it does this (if the claim is correct) should not be accounted a point of weakness in history, but rather one of strength. We can see this by reflecting on the considerations (a) that the ultimate aim of all judgment is to characterise reality in its individual detail, and (b) that abstract sciences (by which we may understand what are normally called *the* sciences in English—i.e. the natural sciences) conspicuously fail to achieve this aim. For, as Descartes saw in discussing scientific method long ago,[2] these sciences do not describe concrete fact but deal in mere possibilities. 'If p, then q' is the form which their conclusions take, and such hypothetical propositions can be formulated, and what is more, can be true, even if there are no actual examples of the connections in question. This is not to deny the obvious truth that the inductive sciences at any rate have a point of contact with reality in that they arise out of, and constantly come back to, reflection on the data of perception. It is to stress rather that the results at which such sciences arrive, just because they purport to state universal connections, are none of them categorically true of fact. In logical language, they are formulated in propositions which lack existential import. They do not state what actually is the case, but what might be if certain conditions were fulfilled.

This account of scientific propositions might well be accepted by philosophers who are generally out of sympathy with the idealist point of view. What of the other part of the theory, that

1. Though not all British idealists would accept it: see pp. 14–15 above.
2. *Discourse on Method*, pt. VI.

history affords us knowledge of the individual? Here we must make clear that a very substantial claim is being made for the historian. It is being asserted, in effect, that historical thinking is not discursive, i.e. does not reach its conclusions by applying general concepts to particular cases, but is, in a certain sense, intuitive. And the basis of the claim is to be found, if the supporters of the theory are to be believed, by considering the special nature of the subject-matter with which history deals.

We have argued above that the proper object of the historian is the doings and experiences of human beings in the past. That thesis was put forward as one which philosophers of all schools ought to accept; but it is only candid to remark that it is particularly congenial to idealists. For, these writers say, the doings and experiences of human beings are the doings and experiences of minds, and we can grasp these in their concrete detail just because we have (or are) minds ourselves. Nature we must look at from the outside, but thoughts and experiences are accessible to us from within. We can grasp them in a unique way because we can re-think or re-live them, imaginatively putting ourselves in the place of the persons, past or present, who first thought or experienced them. This process of imaginative re-living, it is maintained, is central in historical thinking, and explains why that study can give us the individual knowledge which other sciences fail to provide.

The strength of the theory just outlined clearly lies in its apparent correspondence to psychical fact. In our everyday lives we all of us find it possible to put ourselves, to some extent at least, in other people's places, and to enter into their thoughts and feelings by so doing. By this process of sympathetic understanding we are able to penetrate their minds and appreciate why they act as they do. And, on the surface at least, the process is not one of argument. When we see a man in obvious pain, we do not say to ourselves: 'Here is a man whose face is contorted, who utters cries and groans, etc.; persons who do these things are in pain; therefore this man is in pain.' We see that he is in pain *at once*, feel for him *immediately*. And if this is true of our understanding of our contemporaries, it seems natural to extend it, *mutatis mutandis*, to the understanding of past persons' thoughts and experiences, for no difference of principle is involved in the two sets of cases. Here too our understanding seems to be, in a sense, immediate and intuitive: a point which is brought out by our putting imagination high on the list of qualities which a successful historian must possess.

But if the theory thus has an immediate attraction, it must also be admitted that there are obvious objections to it. To say nothing of criticisms of the initial thesis, which we have accepted ourselves, that history is properly concerned with human experiences, we can well ask if apparent correspondence with fact is a sufficient guarantee of the main plank in the idealist platform. Granted that we do appear to feel for others immediately, to enter into their thoughts without explicit argument, is it so certain that no *concealed* inference is involved? If the process is as immediate as some idealists have made out, why does it sometimes lead to false conclusions? And how are we to explain the fact that in psychology, which purports to be *the* science of the mind, success has been achieved only when enquirers have abandoned intuitive methods and approached their subject-matter with the presuppositions of natural science? How too do we explain the occasional emergence of general propositions in historical arguments? Are they there simply because the historians who enunciate them are corrupted by false philosophical theory, or is there a different reason for their presence? Can what has been said about 'retrodiction' above be completely discounted, that process being absorbed without remainder into the sympathetic understanding of which we have spoken?

To these questions the idealist school has its answers, but we shall not discuss them here. Our purpose has been merely to give a preliminary sketch of a theory which stresses the autonomy of historical thinking in a particularly extreme form. We must now turn to consider a very different view.

The origin of this second theory is to be found in nineteenth-century positivism, and it will be convenient to refer to it as the positivist thesis. One of the primary aims of positivism in most of its forms has been to vindicate the unity of science: to show that, apart from purely analytic disciplines like mathematics and formal logic, all branches of knowledge which deserve their name depend on the same basic procedures of observation, conceptual reflection and verification. This programme clearly excludes anything like the idealist account of history, and indeed involves a denial of the view that history is, in any important sense, an autonomous branch of learning. Against this it is contended that procedure in history does not differ in principle from that of natural science. In each case conclusions are reached by appeal to general truths, the only difference being that the historian usually does not, while the scientist does, make the generalisations to which he appeals explicit. At this point we must note a divergence within the positivist school. The old-fashioned positivists, followers of Auguste Comte, whilst agreeing that history was not in the form in which they knew it a science, hoped none the less to raise it to scientific status. That advance was possible, they thought, if historians would turn their attention from individual facts to the principles which they illustrated: if they would abandon mere fact-grubbing and proceed to formulate the lessons or laws of history. When they did this, Comte thought, history would be raised to the scientific level, and would become identical with the science of sociology. But, as we noted before, this suggestion did not commend itself to working historians, and more recent sympathisers with the positivist programme have adopted a different attitude to history. The historian is now allowed (for example, by Sir Karl Popper[1]) to remain preoccupied with particular events, and is not urged to abandon them for higher things, as he was by Comte; but he is granted this concession only at the expense of recognising that history is something less than a science. History is comparable not to the sciences proper but to practical activities like engineering. In each case general knowledge is involved and applied, but in each case the centre of interest is in the particular specimen under examination. And if it is asked what general knowledge is in question, the answer is that that depends on the kind of history. Historians use general knowledge of every kind, trivial and technical, according to their subject-matter. But there is no case where they reach conclusions without appealing to general propositions at all.

The attraction of this view is the attraction of all positivism: its avoidance of mystery-mongering. History, to judge from the way some philosophers speak of it, is a thing about which we all ought to be particularly solemn, since it offers that individual knowledge which other sciences pursue in vain. But the positivist theory, especially in its later form, removes all ground for such solemnity. It sees nothing peculiar in the fact that the historian is concerned

1. See *The Open Society*, vol. II, pp. 248–52, 342–4.

with particular events: so are we all in our daily lives. And it argues that historical understanding involves precisely the same reference to general truths which is made in any deductive argument. Thus historical thinking can be seen to possess no peculiarities of its own, but to be in principle one with scientific thinking. History is not a science, but equally it is not an extra-scientific source of knowledge.

This is no doubt a comforting conclusion to come to, especially if we are scientifically minded. But it may be asked if the reasoning which establishes it is altogether sound. In this connection it is pertinent to note that the whole philosophy of positivism has, paradoxically enough in a school so opposed to metaphysics, a strong *a priori* flavour about it. Having decided in advance that all knowledge must be one, positivists proceed to lay down a formula for what constitutes scientific knowledge and scientific argument, and then to test all existing disciplines by their ability to fit this Procrustes' bed. Some, such as metaphysics and theology, are told they consist of nonsense propositions; history is treated more politely, but still in a somewhat high-handed way. And we may well wonder whether a different approach to the subject, in which we begin not from a general theory but from a scrutiny of the actual procedures of historians, will bear out all the positivists say. On the face of things at least it is not likely that the idealists, many of whom have had personal experience of advanced historical work, are wholly wrong in their view of the subject. But to come to some decision between them and the positivists we must broach the whole subject of historical explanation, and this will demand a chapter to itself.

3

HISTORICAL EXPLANATION

§ 1. *Collingwood's theory of history*

I propose to begin my discussion of this subject with a fuller consideration of the idealist theory of historical thinking briefly sketched towards the end of the last chapter. I do this because the idealists have to offer a bold and clear-cut account of explanation in history, with which anyone who deals with the subject must come to terms. And it is the more necessary for an English writer to pay attention to this theory, in that a form of it was advocated by one of the most lucid and penetrating writers on philosophy of history in the language, R. G. Collingwood. Collingwood did not himself live to complete the large-scale work on the subject which he had planned for many years before his premature death in 1943; but his posthumous book, *The Idea of History*, edited from lectures and papers he left, gives, together with his earlier publications, a fair idea of the view he was trying to establish.

The idealist theory of history, we may begin by remarking, consists in essentials of two propositions. First, that history is, in a sense which remains to be specified, properly concerned with human thoughts and experiences. And second that, just because of this, historical understanding is of a unique and immediate character. The historian, it is maintained, can penetrate to the inner nature of the events he is studying, can grasp them as it were from within. This is an advantage which can never be enjoyed by the natural scientist, who can never know what it is like to be a physical object in the way in which an historian can know what it was like to be Julius Caesar. In Collingwood's words:

> To the scientist, nature is always and merely a 'phenomenon,' not in the sense of being defective in reality, but in the sense of being a spectacle presented to his intelligent observation; whereas the events of history are never mere phenomena, never mere spectacles for contemplation, but things which the historian looks, not at, but through, to discern the thought within them.
>
> (*Idea of History*, p. 214)

History is intelligible in this way because it is a manifestation of mind. Whether nature manifests mind in fact we cannot say: that is a metaphysical question on which no agreement has so far been possible. But at least we know that the natural scientist has to treat it as if it does not. The sterility of ancient and medieval physics proved the practical impossibility of assuming that it did.

Now it should be noticed that, of these two propositions, whilst the second is hardly likely to be true unless the first is, the first can be true even if the second is false. It may be that all history is, in some sense, the history of thought, without its following that historical understanding is unique and immediate. But before we say anything about that we should turn our attention to the first proposition, and in particular to its key-word 'thought.'

When it is said that history is essentially concerned with 'thought,' what is being referred to? The term is capable of both a wider and a narrower meaning, and the ambiguity is reflected in an important division among supporters of the idealist theory. For the German philosopher Wilhelm Dilthey (1833–1911), history, along with e.g. law, economics, literary criticism and sociology, belonged to the group of studies he called sciences of mind (*Geisteswissenschaften*). The characteristic of these studies, which contrasted with the natural sciences (*Naturwissenschaften*), was that their subject-matter could be 'lived through' (*erlebt*) or known from within. Now what can be 'lived through' in Dilthey's sense is human experiences in the widest use of the term: men's feelings, emotions and sensations, as well as their thinkings and reasonings. Hence, for Dilthey, to say that history was properly concerned with human thoughts would be the same as to say it was concerned with human experiences: the word 'thoughts' would be used generically, much as *cogitatio* is in the philosophy of Descartes. Dilthey would have denied that all history is the history of thought if that were understood to mean the history of thinking proper, considering such a conception altogether too narrow and intellectualistic to fit the facts.

But Collingwood, who was certainly familiar with Dilthey's theories, deliberately opted for this narrow view. When *he* said that all history was the history of thought, he meant that it was properly concerned with intellectual operations. All thinking, he explained, took place against a background of feeling and emotion, but it was not with that that the historian was concerned. The historian could not be occupied with that background, because he could not hope to re-live it. It was only thoughts in the strict sense which were capable of resurrection, and so only thoughts could constitute the subject-matter of history.

The reader may well be puzzled to know what led Collingwood to maintain so apparently extreme and paradoxical a theory as this, and it will perhaps be worth our while to look at the contrasting views more closely.

Dilthey supported his theory of the autonomy of the *Geisteswissenschaften* with an account of how mental operations are known. At the centre of this were his concepts of 'expression' and 'understanding.' According to him, all our mental experiences —feelings, emotions, thinking—tend to get some sort of external expression. Thinking, for example, is normally accompanied by spoken or written words or other symbols, grief by one sort of facial expression and bodily behaviour, joy by another, and so on. The process of understanding the minds of other people, and for that matter part of the process of understanding our own minds, is one of interpreting these expressions. But Dilthey was emphatic that it was not a process of inference. We pass *directly*, he appears to think, from awareness of the expression to awareness of that which it expresses; or rather, though we do not get at the original experience itself, we have in ourselves an experience precisely like it. Thus when I see someone showing all the signs of pain I am immediately pained myself. I know what it is like to be the man in question because my mental state corresponds exactly to his.

Two criticisms can be made of this account. First, it can be

asked why, if Dilthey is right in thinking the process to be immediate and not inferential, we sometimes get it wrong. That we do
often misread people's thoughts and feelings could not be denied;
and it seems most natural to say that when we do we draw the
wrong conclusions from the evidence at our disposal—the expressions of which Dilthey speaks. In that case the process is, after all,
one of inference. And secondly, it may be suggested that Dilthey's
theory leads to a fundamentally sceptical position. If we can never
get at the actual experience which gave rise to a certain expression,
how do we know that our own experience is, as he assures us,
precisely like it? It looks as if Dilthey was involved here in the
common difficulties of the representative theory of knowledge, and
had not sufficiently considered how to avoid them.

Collingwood felt the force of both these points, though he was
in general sympathy with Dilthey's point of view and alive to the
great importance for history of the theory of expression. But he
wanted to avoid scepticism about historical knowledge and, as
part of that, to avoid having to say that we can make only more
or less well-founded guesses about other people's minds, including
the minds of past persons. And the only way he saw of achieving
this result was to argue that all we could know of them was their
thinkings and reasonings in the strict sense.

That we could know so much he maintained on the ground that
acts of thought, as opposed to the felt background against which
they took place, were intrinsically capable of revival after an
interval. If, for example, I began to think about a subject which I
had not considered for years, I might (though I should not always)
succeed in reviving my previous thoughts about it, though my
thinking now would have a different background of emotion and
feeling from what it had then; and if I thought about the history of
Julius Caesar I might succeed in reviving his thoughts too. The
fact that Caesar's thoughts had not previously constituted part of
my mental history was no obstacle to this: there was, Collingwood
said, 'no tenable theory of personal identity' preventing the same
act of thought from falling within two different mental series. Hence
a history confined strictly to the history of thinking was a perfectly
feasible enterprise, though one understood in a wide sense was not.[1]

1. For the difficult argument cf. *The Idea of History*, pp. 282 ff; and pp. 90–2
below.

Accordingly for Collingwood the central concept of history is the concept of action, i.e. of thought expressing itself in external behaviour. Historians have, he believed, to start from the merely physical or from descriptions of the merely physical; but their aim is to penetrate behind these to the thought which underlay them. Thus they may start from the bare fact that a person (or, more strictly, a body) called Julius Caesar on a certain day in 49 B.C. crossed the River Rubicon with such-and-such forces. But they are not content to stop there; they want to go on and find out what was in Caesar's mind, what thought lay behind those bodily movements. In Collingwood's own terminology, they want to pass from the 'outside' of the event to its 'inside.' And once they make that transition, he claims, the action becomes for them fully intelligible:

> For history, the object to be discovered is not the mere event, but the thought expressed in it. To discover that thought is already to understand it. After the historian has ascertained the facts, there is no further process of inquiring into the causes. When he knows what happened, he already knows why it happened.
>
> (*Idea of History*, p. 214)

If I know what Nelson did at the battle of Trafalgar, to use a favourite example of Collingwood's, I also know why he did it, because I make his thoughts mine and pass from one to another as I should in my own thinking. I have no need of any general knowledge of the behaviour of admirals in sea battles to attain this understanding. It is not, in fact, a matter of discursive, but of immediate knowledge. But it is only this because thought, and thought alone, is in question.

§ 2. *Criticisms of Collingwood's theory*

We may agree to take Collingwood's version of the idealist theory as its standard form for our present purposes, and must now proceed to comment on it. I shall concentrate first on what he has to say about the central importance for history of the conception of action, and on his description of the historian's procedure as being the re-thinking of past thoughts.

Exception may be taken to these views on various grounds.

Thus (a) supporters of materialist theories of historical interpretation would certainly ridicule them as implying a ludicrous neglect of the natural background to historical events. To say that all history is the history of thought is to suggest at least that men make their own history, free of determination by natural forces; and what could be more absurd? But this criticism sounds more devastating than it in fact is. We have only to remember that the thought of which Collingwood is talking is thought in action, not the thought of abstract speculation, to turn its edge. Why should we suppose him to have been unaware that such thought develops out of, and in response to, a background of natural as well as human forces? His theory would certainly be silly if it neglected that fact; but have we any reason to suppose that it does?

(b) Passing this point by, we may next consider the criticism that Collingwood's view would only hold water if all human actions were deliberate, when so many of them clearly are not. What the historian has to do, he tells us, is to penetrate from the external event to the thought which constituted it and re-think that thought. But a great many actions which history investigates were done on the spur of the moment, in response to a sudden impulse; and how Collingwood's programme is to be carried out in regard to these is not immediately obvious.

(c) With this criticism we may connect another, that the theory is plausible only so long as certain types of history are considered. So long as we concentrate our attention on biography, political and military history, it sounds reasonable enough; but if we pass to the consideration of, for example, economic history, it becomes very much more difficult to apply. Is it at all illuminating to say that one who deals with, e.g., the history of prices is essentially concerned with human actions, and that his proper business is to re-think the thoughts of the agents who did them? What actions and whose thoughts are in question here?

Of these two objections, the first can perhaps be met with the reflection that much action which is impulsive and, to that extent, seems 'thoughtless,' can none the less be shown on further investigation to be the expression of thought. If I strike a man in a fit of passion my action is certainly not deliberate; but it would be idle to deny that there was, as we say, an idea behind it. I wanted to hit the man and express my displeasure, however little I had an

explicit plan before my mind. And it can be contended with fair
plausibility that the historian in studying impulsive acts and
seeking to uncover the thoughts behind them has a task
which compares at some points with that of the psycho-analyst,
whose success in revealing carefully worked out plans behind
apparently irrational actions is surely relevant to the subject we are
considering.

The force of the other objection, too, depends on the assumption
that the theory will work only if the thoughts spoken of are
embodied in deliberate acts of thinking occurring in the minds of
single agents. The actions with which economic history deals are
the actions of innumerable agents—in fact, all those who take part
in the economic processes under investigation. And the thoughts
which the economic historian tries to get at are expressed, often
enough, in complicated series of actions carried out by different
persons over long stretches of time, few, if any, of whom are aware
of the direction of the whole movement. It may well be impossible
to detect any deliberate plan here; but is that an insuperable objection
to the idealist theory? Surely there is nothing very revolutionary in
the suggestion that an idea can be persistently influential without
being continuously before anyone's mind: it can have, as it were,
a background effect, being assumed unconsciously by persons who
have never explicitly thought about it. And I do not see why this
should not apply to the sphere of economic as much as it does to,
say, that of political or cultural history.

The force of both criticisms derives from the mistaken identification of what a person has *in mind* with what he has *before his mind*.
It is falsely believed that when we say that historians have to
penetrate to the thoughts behind men's overt actions we imply
that every action has two parts: first thinking and then physical
doing. The difficulties we have been discussing then arise, as there
clearly are many cases which the form suggested just will not fit.
But though Collingwood's language in this context (in particular,
his emphasis on the need for *re-thinking* past thoughts) is not free
from ambiguity, it is not essential to interpret him as having made
this objectionable assumption. It makes sense to speak of discovering the thought behind a physical act even in cases where thinking
did *not* precede overt action; and indeed we often attempt to do this
sort of thing in everyday life, for example in the law courts.

(d) This must also be our answer to the frontal attack on the inner/outer dichotomy as applied to action delivered by Professor Ryle in *The Concept of Mind*.[1] Professor Ryle objects to this terminology on the ground that if we speak *both* of a man's overt doings *and* of the thoughts they express, and argue that it is the business of the historian to pass from the former to the latter, we set him an impossible task, since the thoughts here spoken of are, by definition, private to the person who has them and accessible to no-one else. In so doing we involve ourselves in the traditional philosophical problem of our knowledge of other minds, a problem which cannot be solved satisfactorily for the simple reason that it rests on a gross misunderstanding. If we will only recognise that, as Professor Ryle puts it, 'overt intelligent performances are not clues to the working of minds; they are those workings,'[2] misunderstanding and problem disappear together.

But the inner/outer terminology can be defended without accepting the implications Professor Ryle ascribes to its supporters. It can be accepted on the respectable ground that it is empirically illuminating: that it does represent something that historians, lawyers, politicians and ordinary men do in the course of their normal thinking. Sometimes (very often, so far as history is concerned) they find themselves confronted with a bare record of the physical doings of certain agents; and in these circumstances they set themselves to discover the ideas or thoughts or intentions which the agents in question had, whether explicitly or not, 'in mind.' To say that in these circumstances they are trying to move from the 'outer' to the 'inner' aspect of an action or set of actions is to employ a metaphor which may be dangerously misleading for philosophers; but it would not mislead any historian or man of affairs who kept his wits about him. For after all it is the sort of thing we all of us do in following current events in the political world, when we ask, for example, what Stalin is 'thinking of' in sending Vyshinsky to Washington, or speculate on what 'lies behind' the more or less well-attested physical fact that large bodies of Russian troops are moving east to west across Poland.

What Professor Ryle has done is bring out in a striking way the

1. pp. 56–58.
2. op cit., p. 58.

misleading character of Collingwood's language of 're-thinking,' which is inadequate for the purposes for which it is intended. The historian has certainly to do more than re-think the thoughts which were explicitly before the minds of those whose actions he studies, even in cases where the acts were deliberate. Historical characters, as Hegel pointed out, often accomplish (and for that matter attempt) more than they know, and this must be allowed for in any tenable account of historical thinking. But I think myself that the allowance can be made inside the context of the idealist theory without destroying that theory's main contentions.[1]

What this comes to is that we ought, despite Professor Ryle, to accept the idealist theory of expression as substantially correct. We remarked earlier that it was hardly likely that the idealists, who have a good deal of genuine historical work to their credit (Dilthey, Croce and Collingwood, to name only three, were all experienced historians), had wholly misconceived the nature of historical thinking; and the point is supported by the present case. Whatever our view of the rest of their theory, we cannot deny that the idealists have rightly emphasised the difference between the attitude a natural scientist adopts towards the facts he investigates and that taken up by historians towards their evidence.

The difference is well put by Collingwood, in a passage already quoted, where he speaks of historians looking not at, but through, historical phenomena, to discern the thought within them. We can illustrate it, again following Collingwood, by comparing the procedure of a palaeontologist with that of an archaeologist towards their respective 'finds'. The former takes his remains as evidence enabling him to reconstruct the physical appearance and character-istics of the animals whose bones they are, and to work out the evolution of species now extinct. But the latter, when he discovers remains of a settlement or a camp, is not content with recon-structing the physical appearance it must have presented when actually occupied; he wants further to use it as evidence throwing

1. [The trouble is more deep-seated than is here recognised, as Mr A. C. Danto has made clear in chapter VIII of his *Analytical Philosophy of History*. Danto remarks on the frequency in history of 'narrative sentences' like 'Aristarchus anticipated Copernicus' which describe events in the light of their outcome; as he says, reference to what the agents had in mind could never be an adequate basis for such descriptions. I make some complementary points in the article cited on p. 63.]

light on the thoughts and experiences of the people who lived or
fought there. To put the point another way, whereas nature is all
on the surface (as Goethe cryptically remarked, it has 'neither
shell nor kernel'), history has both inside and outside. And it is
with its inside that historians are properly concerned.

But though we are thus prepared to defend the first part of the
idealist theory, it does not follow that we accept the whole idealist
account of historical explanation. To say that historians must
penetrate behind the phenomena they study is one thing; to hold
that such penetration is achieved by an intuitive act is something
very different.

Can we find any reason for accepting so extravagant a view?
Collingwood, as we have seen, confined the sympathetic understanding which Dilthey had been prepared to extend to all mental
experiences to acts of thinking in the strict sense; but I doubt if
we can follow him even in that. When he tells us that a study of the
evidence will enable us to grasp in a single act both what Nelson
thought at Trafalgar and why he thought it, and that this knowledge is achieved without reference to any general propositions
about the behaviour of admirals, we may well wonder whether he
has not been deceived by his own example. We feel that there is
no major difficulty about the doctrine when it is applied to persons
like Nelson and Julius Caesar, because we assume all too easily
that Nelson and Julius Caesar were men like ourselves. But if we
try to apply it to the actions of an African witch-doctor or a Viking
chief, we may well begin to have serious doubts about it. To make
anything of the behaviour of such persons, we should all be inclined
to say, we need something more than sympathetic understanding;
we need experience, first- or second-hand, of the ways in which
they commonly react to the situations in which they find themselves.

But for an idealist to admit this is to give his whole case away,
for that experience reduces to awareness, explicit or implicit, of
certain *general* truths. What is being said, in fact, is that the process
of interpreting the behaviour in question is one of inference in the
ordinary sense. And if this applies to unfamiliar cases like that of
the witch-doctor, should it not apply to familiar cases too? Is it not
true that our understanding of Nelson depends in an important
way on our knowing something about the conduct of sea battles

generally? If we had no such knowledge, should we understand his actions at all?

I conclude that Collingwood's main thesis will not bear examination. It is not true that we grasp and understand the thought of past persons in a single act of intuitive insight. We have to discover what they were thinking, and find out why they thought it, by interpreting the evidence before us, and this process of interpretation is one in which we make at least implicit reference to general truths. The historian certainly has to do something different from the scientist, but he has no special powers of insight to help him carry out the task. He needs imagination in a large degree, but he needs experience too. To suggest that he can do his job by putting himself in the place of the persons he studies, whilst appearing to answer to the facts, is not ultimately illuminating. For the process of putting oneself in another's place is itself susceptible of further analysis.

I shall be dealing later with some further problems arising out of the preceding discussion, which bears on the question of historical truth no less than on that of historical explanation. For the present I need only add the remark that the rejection of Collingwood's version of the theory removes any incentive there was for accepting his very narrow definition of the field of history. Collingwood himself proposed to confine history to thought proper because he believed that thinking alone could be understood in his peculiar sense: it was only of thinking that we could have individual and direct knowledge. But we have seen reasons for rejecting his view, and can therefore go back without hesitation to the wider formula from which we started—that history is concerned with the doings and experiences of human beings in the past. The historian, we shall continue to say, does try to resurrect the thought of the past; but he is interested not solely in ideas proper, but also in the background of feeling and emotion which those ideas had. When he attempts to uncover the spirit of an age, it is not merely its intellectual life he hopes to penetrate: he wants to get at its emotional life too. No doubt, as Collingwood saw, there are difficulties in his carrying out the task, but they apply to both parts of it. If historical scepticism is justified, it applies to thought as well as to feeling.[1]

1. [For criticisms of this interpretation of Collingwood, see the additional note at the end of this chapter.]

§ 3. 'Colligation' in history

The position now reached is that we have rejected the main contention of the idealists about historical explanation and argued that it involves some sort of reference to general truths. This may seem to commit us without further ado to some form of the positivist thesis (above, pp. 45–7). But before accepting that conclusion we ought perhaps to take a closer look at the actual practice of historians. If we do that we cannot help being struck by their use of a procedure which fits the idealist better than the positivist theory, the procedure of explaining an event by tracing its intrinsic relations to other events and locating it in its historical context. This is the process which was described in our introductory chapter as one of 'colligation', and it will certainly be worth our while to consider its nature and importance.

If an historian is asked to explain a particular historical event I think he is often inclined to begin his explanation by saying that the event in question is to be seen as part of a general movement which was going on at the time. Thus Hitler's reoccupation of the Rhineland in 1936 might be elucidated by reference to the general policy of German self-assertion and expansion which Hitler pursued from the time of his accession to power. Mention of this policy, and specification of earlier and later steps in carrying it out, such as the repudiation of unilateral disarmament, the German withdrawal from the League of Nations, the absorption of Austria and the incorporation of the Sudetenland, do in fact serve to render the isolated action from which we started more intelligible. And they do it by enabling us to locate that action in its context, to see it as a step in the realisation of a more or less consistent policy. To grasp a policy of that sort and appreciate the way in which individual events contributed to its realisation is, at least in many cases, part of what is normally involved in giving an historical explanation.

Now it is important to realise that the historian's ability to use this form of explanation depends on the special nature of his subject-matter. It is only because of his concern, rightly stressed by the idealists, with actions, that he can think in this way at all. It is the fact that every action has a thought-side which makes the whole thing possible. Because actions are, broadly speaking, the realisation of purposes, and because a single purpose or policy can find expression in a whole series of actions, whether carried out by one person or by several, we can say in an intelligible sense that some historical events are intrinsically related. They are so related because the series of actions in question forms a whole of which it is true to say not only that the later members are determined by the earlier, but also that the determination is reciprocal, the earlier members themselves being affected by the fact that the later ones were envisaged. This is a situation which we do not meet with in nature,[1] natural events having, for scientific purposes at any rate, no 'insides', and therefore admitting only of extrinsic connections.

The point we are making is that historical thinking, because of the nature of the historian's subject-matter, often proceeds in teleological terms. But to this it will be objected that it tends to make history far more deliberate and tidy than it in fact is. Certainly historians speak of general movements which characterise particular ages: the Enlightenment, the Romantic movement, the age of reform in nineteenth-century England, the rise of monopoly capitalism. But can it be held with any plausibility that these movements are in every case deliberate attempts to give expression to a coherent policy? Of many of them at least any such claim would be palpably untrue. No doubt there are some movements in history— that for legal reform in Great Britain in the early years of the last century would be an example—which are, in essentials, deliberate attempts to carry out a previously formulated programme; but they seem to be the exception rather than the rule in history. For evidence on the other side we have only to ask who planned the rise of monopoly capitalism or the Romantic movement itself.

The force of this objection must at once be admitted. It would be absurd to explain history on the assumption that it consisted of a series of deliberately planned happenings. Men are not so calculating as that, and even if they did try to act in every case according to some carefully formulated policy they would find that circumstances, human and natural, were sometimes too much for them. But I think all this can be admitted without sacrificing the main point of our theory.

For, first, if it is absurd to look on history as a series of deliberate

---

1. The existence of organic bodies appears to give the lie to this statement. But even if (as mechanistic biologists would deny) we cannot explain these without introducing the concept of purpose, it is clearly impossible to regard their behaviour as purposive *in the same sense* as human behaviour is.

movements, it is equally absurd to ignore the truth that men do sometimes pursue coherent policies. The Nazis did, after all, plan to conquer Europe, and no history of the years from 1933 to 1945 could fail to mention their plan. A straightforward teleological explanation is thus entirely justified for some historical events. And, secondly, though it is often impossible to have recourse to such an explanation in its simple form, the very fact that historians try to group historical events together under movements and general tendencies shows that they hanker after some substitute for it. If they cannot think in plain teleological terms, they still use a procedure which is semi-teleological. They do, in fact, explain events by pointing to ideas which they embody and citing other events with which they are intimately connected, even though they know that many of the agents concerned had little if any conscious awareness of the ideas in question. And their justification for doing this is the fact, already noted, that ideas can exert an influence on people's conduct even when they are not continuously before the minds of the persons who act on them. Thus the idea of Great Britain's having an imperial mission, though explicitly advocated by only a small minority of persons in the country at the time, came towards the end of the Victorian era to exercise a most important influence on the conduct of British foreign policy, and no account of that policy could afford to leave it unmentioned. There was, in fact, a recognisable imperialist phase in British political history, even though the policy of imperialism was not consciously accepted or deliberately pursued by the majority of those in power at the time.

It seems clear to me that this process of 'colligating' events under 'appropriate conceptions', to use Whewell's terms, does form an important part of historical thinking, and I should myself connect it with what was said at the beginning of the last chapter about the historian's aim to make a coherent whole out of the events he studies. His way of doing that, I suggest, is to look for certain dominant concepts or leading ideas by which to illuminate his facts, to trace connections between those ideas themselves, and then to show how the detailed facts become intelligible in the light of them by constructing a 'significant' narrative of the events of the period in question. No doubt this programme is one which, in any concrete case, can be carried out with only partial success:

both the right key ideas and insight into their application to the detailed facts may elude us, whilst the intelligibility sought for can only be intelligibility within an arbitrarily delimited period (unless the historian marks off a set of events for study he cannot even start colligating them). But these admissions do not alter the main point, that the process is one which historians do use, and that therefore any account of historical explanation should find a place for it.

It is, however, easy to overestimate the significance of the process I have been describing, and it may quieten the suspicions of some readers if I end my discussion with some remarks on that point. I must make clear, first, that to say that we explain historical events by referring to the ideas they embody is not to hold that history is a rational process in any disputable sense; and, second, that I am not maintaining that this is the only explanatory procedure adopted by historians.

(a) I explained before that colligation fitted the idealist better than the positivist view of history (it is obviously connected with the thesis that all history is of thought), and suspicious persons will undoubtedly see in my advocacy of it an attempt to reintroduce idealism. What are your dominant concepts, I shall be asked, but Hegel's concrete universals in disguise, and what is the attempt to show history to be an intelligible whole but a revival of a now discredited rationalism? I should like to make clear that it is nothing of the sort. In saying that the historian attempts to find intelligibility in history by colligating events according to appropriate ideas I am suggesting no theory of the ultimate moving forces in history. I say nothing about the *origin* of the ideas on which the historian seizes; it is enough for me that those ideas were influential at the time of which he writes. Thus the only rationality in the historical process which my theory assumes is a kind of surface rationality: the fact that this, that and the other event can be grouped together as parts of a single policy or general movement. Of the wider question whether the policy or movement was itself the product of reason in a further sense I have nothing here to say.

It follows that my theory is not rationalistic in what might well be considered a bad sense, but rather one that can be accepted by writers of all schools (I do not see why even Marxists should deny it). But this in itself suggests that colligation needs to be supplemented by further processes if historical explanation is to be complete.

(b) An explanation of historical events in terms of ideas can be no more than partial, if only because it says nothing on such important questions as why those ideas were adopted (what gave them their peculiar appeal) and how far their advocates managed, in the face of natural and human obstacles, to put them into effect. A complete account must clearly raise these matters, but the colligation theory passes them by, concentrating solely on the content of the act it studies. There is nothing vicious in its doing this, so long as the abstraction is recognised; trouble comes only when this qualification is ignored, and the theory, or something like it, is put forward as the whole truth. It is then that we fall into the extravagances of the idealists examined above. But we need fall into no such absurdities if we keep the full facts in mind.

To what other process of explanation, besides colligation, do historians make appeal? It seems clear that it must be to explanation of a quasi-scientific type, involving the application of general principles to particular cases. Thus we come back, as we did at the end of our discussion of idealism, to something like the positivist theory of historical thinking. In the rest of this chapter we must undertake an examination of the reference to general propositions in history which that theory makes central, and which it seems that any account must acknowledge.[1]

§ 4. *History and knowledge of human nature*

We are agreed that to understand an historical situation we must bring some general knowledge to bear on it, and the first question to ask here is clearly in what this general knowledge consists. Modern positivists, as we saw before, have a simple answer to give. It is that there is no special set of generalisations to which historians make appeal, since the general knowledge needed varies from one historical situation to another. Thus an historian dealing with large-scale movements of population will have recourse, amongst other truths, to the findings of the geographer and the economist. A student of the history of classical scholarship must know something of the chemistry of inks and of paper. A biographer must be

1. [I now have a further discussion of the subject of this section in 'Colligatory Concepts in History', printed in *Studies in the Nature and Teaching of History*, Ed. W. H. Burston and D. Thompson (1967).]

acquainted with psychological laws; and so on. Each type of historian has his particular kind of interests, and each must bring the appropriate general knowledge to bear.

This theory is connected with the view, often put forward by supporters of the positivist school, that it is misleading to speak of history at all as the name of a specific study. There is no such thing as history in the abstract; there are only different kinds of history. History is a generic term, and the genus is real only in its species— political history, military history, economic history, history of language, of art, of science, and so forth. To ask what general propositions history *as such* presupposes is thus to ask a question which it is unprofitable to pursue because it cannot be answered.

That this diffusionist account of history, as it might be called, is plausible and attractive, especially to an age which has little taste for synoptic views of any kind, could scarcely be denied. Its positive contentions at least seem above reproach. Certainly it is the case that there are many different kinds of history, and certainly the exponent of each branch needs specialist knowledge to carry out his task. No doubt, too, abstraction of some kind is a necessary part of the process of acquiring historical knowledge: all actual histories are departmental in the important sense that they look at the past from a certain point of view and concentrate on limited aspects of it. But though all this must be admitted, I doubt myself whether the positivist conclusion follows. For it seems to me that in historical work of all kinds there is a single overriding aim: to build up an intelligible picture of the human past as a concrete whole, so that it comes alive for us in the same way as the lives of ourselves and our contemporaries. Different types of history contribute to this fundamental design in different ways, but I think that all historians do have it in mind. They all hope to throw light on the past of man, and would not have undertaken their particular study if they did not believe that it did that in some degree at least.

Now if there is anything in this contention, it follows that, in addition to the specific generalisations which historians assume, each for his particular purposes, there is also for each a fundamental set of judgments on which all his thinking rests. These judgments concern human nature: they are judgments about the characteristic responses human beings make to the various challenges set them in the course of their lives, whether by the natural conditions in which they live or by their fellow human beings. No doubt some of them are so trivial as to be scarcely worth formulating: no one, for instance, needs to set out formally the truth that men who undergo great physical privations are for the most part lacking in mental energy. But that the body of propositions as a whole is extremely important is shown by the reflection that it is in the light of his conception of human nature that the historian must finally decide both what to accept as fact and how to understand what he does accept. What he takes to be credible depends on what he conceives to be humanly possible, and it is with this that the judgments here in question are concerned. The science of human nature is thus the discipline which is basic for every branch of history. The results of other branches of learning are required for this kind of history or that, but none is of such general importance as the study just named.

§ 5. *Difficulties in this conception*

But if so much is granted, it must also be agreed that the whole subject of the historian's knowledge and use of these judgments about human nature contains many difficulties. And since these difficulties are clearly relevant not only to the question of historical explanation, but also to that of the objectivity of historical statements, it will be necessary to discuss them at some length.

To begin with, there is the problem of how the historian comes by these basic beliefs. The obvious answer here would be 'from the recognised authorities on the subject,' i.e. from those who make it their business to study human nature in the modern sciences of psychology and sociology. But the puzzle is that there are plenty of competent historians, men whose judgment of particular historical situations can be trusted, who are largely ignorant of those sciences, their methods and results. They apparently know a great deal about human nature and can make good use of their knowledge, though they have never made a formal study of the human mind or of the general characteristics of human society.

From what other source could they have derived their knowledge? The only alternative answer would seem to be 'from experience'. And this is an answer which some philosophers would

c

certainly find congenial. The understanding of human nature shown by historians, they would say, is not different from that which we all display in our daily lives, and comes from the same source. It is part of that vague amalgam of currently recognised generalities, derived from common experience and more or less confirmed by our own, which we all accept for everyday purposes and know by the name of 'common sense.' Now the merits of this second answer should not be in doubt. If it can be accepted, any mystery there may be in the subject we are considering vanishes. We need no longer trouble ourselves about the significance of the historian's understanding of human nature, since the categories of history turn out to be identical with those of common sense. There can be no pretence, in these circumstances, that historical knowledge is worthy of special remark or can lay any peculiar claim to philosophical scrutiny.

That the historian's understanding of human nature is derived in some way from experience, and even that it is continuous with what we call common-sense knowledge, I should not wish to deny. But I doubt whether we can leave the matter at that without doing less than justice to the subtlety and depth of insight into the possibilities of human nature shown by the great historians. One of the characteristics of such persons is that they succeed in going far beyond common sense in their appreciation and understanding of human situations. Their powers of imagination or intuition, as they might even be called, open up unsuspected possibilities for their readers, enabling them to penetrate the minds of ages very different from their own. In this respect, as in some others, their work bears a close resemblance to that of great writers in other fields. Creative literature, too, in particular the drama and the novel, requires in its exponents an insight into the possibilities of human nature which is peculiarly intense; and here too the insight is seldom come by as the result of formal study. And though it is no doubt true to say that it rests in each case on the writer's experience and on the common experience of his time, that statement is not really very illuminating.[1] For we are left when we think about it with the awkward question why some can make so much of their

---

1. I should say the same of the suggestion that this knowledge is all, in Professor Ryle's antithesis (*The Concept of Mind*, ch. II), to be classified as 'knowledge how' as opposed to 'knowledge that.'

experience and others so little. Is experience enough to explain the many-sided appreciation of human nature shown by a Shakespeare or a Tolstoy? Can it account for the wonderful conviction Emily Brontë managed to impart to the character of Heathcliff, a creature whose like neither she nor her readers can have met with in real life, but who nevertheless strikes us as entirely credible? To say that all that is required to account for literary understanding is common sense and common experience is clearly to fall short of the truth: genius is wanted too. And though the average historian can fulfil his function adequately enough with qualities amounting to no more than those of sharpened common sense, it can surely be argued that something like genius is required for really telling work in this field too.

I conclude that there is a genuine problem about the historian's knowledge of human nature, and suggest that it is closely akin to that raised by literary work and the appreciation of literature. But I must leave the problem without discussion, and pass on to a further point of difficulty about the science of human nature.

This point concerns the variability of the basic propositions of the science. We have said already that it is in the light of his conception of human nature that the historian must ultimately decide what to accept as fact. But conceptions of human nature, when we reflect on the matter, vary in the most striking way from age to age. What seems normal at one time (e.g. the Middle Ages) appears quite abnormal at another (e.g. the eighteenth century), and the difference is often so profound that the earlier age becomes positively incomprehensible to the later. Hence the misunderstandings which mar the pages of a writer like Gibbon when he deals with questions of religion. Nor must it be thought that such misunderstandings belong only to the past, and that we are wiser than our predecessors. No doubt we are more conscious than Gibbon and Voltaire were that there are differences between our own times and past ages; but it does not follow that we are fully successful in overcoming the differences. And indeed it seems unreasonable to expect that we should be, for we could only do it if we could step outside our own time and contemplate the past *sub specie aeternitatis*.

Now a science whose basic propositions vary in this way may well be thought no science at all; and the conclusion has in fact been drawn. Collingwood, for example, frequently asserted that

there are no 'eternal' truths about human nature, only truths about
the ways in which human beings behaved at this epoch or that.
There are no eternal truths about human nature, he argued, because
human nature is constantly changing. But we need to scrutinise
this apparently plausible assertion with some care. When it is said
that human nature changes from age to age, are we meant to
conclude that there is *no* identity between past and present, no
continuous development from one to the other, but that the two
are sheerly different? And if we are (as Collingwood himself
suggested in his more sceptical moments), does not that rule out
the possibility of any intelligent understanding of the past? If men
in ancient Greece or the Middle Ages, for example, had nothing in
common with men in the world today, how could we hope to make
anything of their experiences? An attempt to do so would be like
trying to read a cypher text of which it was laid down in advance
that the solution must elude us.

This in itself is no more than an *ad hominem* argument: it does
not *prove* that there is something constant in human nature, and
therefore that a science of human nature is possible. It merely calls
attention to the fact that we think we can understand past ages, just
as we think we can understand our contemporaries. But the conviction is at any rate supported when we reflect that wholesale
scepticism about historical understanding would entail wholesale
scepticism about literary understanding too. If we cannot understand people's actions in the past, we cannot hope to make anything
of their literature either. Yet we certainly do think we can, to some
extent at least, though we should agree that some writers are more
readily intelligible to us than others, and that some literary productions continue to baffle us for all our efforts to interpret them.

It might thus be argued that a science of human nature is possible
in principle, despite the apparent variations in behaviour and
beliefs from one age to another. But even if that is so, it should not
give rise to any false optimism about historical understanding. It
still remains true that different historians bring to their work
different conceptions of how men do and (perhaps we should add)
should behave, and that this fact has a most important effect on the
results they achieve. We are not concerned here to explore the
further implications of the fact[1]: our aim has been only to point

1. For some further implications, see Chapter 5 below.

out its relevance to the subject of historical explanation. That it is both relevant and important I should say myself was beyond doubt.

There is one further difficulty about the science of human nature to which I shall refer briefly in conclusion (its connection with the two previous points should be clear enough). I have argued that truths about human nature are *presupposed* in historical understanding, and spoken of the historian's *approaching* his work with a certain conception of the nature of man. But the matter cannot be left at that. For, when we come to think about it, it is not only true that we bring to the understanding of history certain notions about the possibilities of human behaviour: we also revise our notions of that subject in the course of our historical work. Thus in reading an account of the doings of persons pretty remote from ourselves, such as the barbarians who broke up the Roman Empire, we start with certain criteria by which to judge and interpret their behaviour; but our reading may very soon induce us to alter these criteria in important respects, by opening our eyes to possibilities we had not suspected. The case of history is here again parallel to that of literature. A great novel or a great play is often said to teach us something about ourselves; yet, as we have seen, we need to bring to it certain pre-existing beliefs about the nature of man.

It is not sufficient, I suspect, to dispose of this point by saying that there is nothing surprising in it, for the simple reason that our knowledge of human nature rests on experience, and is subject to constant revision as our experience is widened. No doubt it is, but the fact remains that our notions on this subject still appear to contain an element which is not due to experience, but may be called *a priori* or subjective according to taste. The existence of this subjective element constitutes a major puzzle for philosophy of history, and is indeed the main cause of the hesitation which many ordinary people would feel if invited to agree that history is capable of becoming a fully scientific study.

We must leave these questions, to which we shall return, and attempt to bring together the results of a long and difficult discussion. We began our consideration of the nature of explanation in history with two views in mind: one which insisted that historical understanding is immediate and intuitive, the other reducing it, in effect, to a sub-form of the thinking of the empirical sciences and likening its procedure to that of common sense. We saw reason to reject the first of these views decisively; but that did not commit us to straightforward acceptance of the second. For though the idealist school went too far in its claims, we saw that it was not wrong in making the concept of action central for the historian, and it was with this that we proposed to connect the teleological, or semi-teleological, procedures which, it was argued, historians follow whatever their views of the ultimate moving forces in history. We recognised, however, that this process of colligating historical events, whilst of great importance, could not constitute the whole nature of historical explanation.[1] Reference to general truths, as in explanations of the scientific type, was also needed, and here we found ourselves in general agreement with the positivist point of view. But we differed from the positivists in holding that a fundamental set of generalisations, belonging to the science of human nature, is presupposed in all historical work; and we tried, in conclusion, to point out certain difficulties which arise about these generalisations and the historian's knowledge of them. Our general result can be summarised by saying that history is, in our view, a form of knowledge with features peculiar to itself, though it is not so different from natural science or even common sense as it has sometimes been thought to be.

Additional note to Chapter 3

Professor A. Donagan, in an article entitled 'The Verification of Historical Theses' (*Philosophical Quarterly*, July 1956), disputes the interpretation of Collingwood's views on history given here and by other critics and says that neither his theory nor his historical practice commit him to the belief that in history past thoughts are infallibly intuited. Collingwood's dictum that all history is the history of thought should be taken as an attempt to bring out the conceptual structure of historical knowledge rather than as an account of what historians do. I should wish myself to stress that

---

1. A further way of bringing this out would be to say that historians who concentrate on tracing general movements in history are primarily occupied with intentions or purposes, whilst a complete explanation of any given action obviously requires reference to causes and motives as well. I agree with Professor Ryle (*The Concept of Mind*, ch. IV) that to find the motive of an action is to classify it as being of a certain type.

Collingwood's aim was to lay bare the peculiar character of historical knowledge, and would admit that his doctrine could be reconstructed without any reference being made to intuition, along the lines followed in Chapter V of Professor W. Dray's *Laws and Explanation in History*. Dray there shows that historians are often concerned with what he calls 'the rationale of actions', and that in this work they bring to bear not generalisations about past behaviour but 'principles of action,' rules which (they suppose) were adopted as expressing 'the thing to do' by the characters with which they are concerned. If it were suggested, however, that this clears up the matter I should want to make three comments. (1) Although on Dray's account an historian does not need to scrutinise analogous cases in order to deduce principles of action, he does need some general knowledge which goes beyond the particular case. To discover the principles on which Nelson was acting at Trafalgar I must at least know that he was present there in the capacity of admiral, and know what an admiral is. (2) Collingwood makes the negative point that (this sort of) historical understanding does not depend on knowledge of general laws, but says little or nothing about what it does consist in. The inference that he thought it must be immediate is entirely natural, more particularly when we remember what he says elsewhere about scientific knowledge being abstract. (3) The fact that Collingwood believed that only past thoughts, and not past feelings, could be re-enacted shows his preoccupation with the issue of historical scepticism; it seems hard to avoid the conclusion that his solution to this was to say that thoughts alone could be grasped without possibility of mistake. I should, however, no longer wish to rely on the passage from *The Idea of History* quoted on p. 52 above to show that Collingwood believed thought to be self-explanatory, as Donagan has convinced me that the word 'it' at the end of the second sentence was intended to refer back to 'event' in the first. See further Mr Dray's article, 'Historical Understanding as Re-thinking,' in *University of Toronto Quarterly*, January 1958.

4

TRUTH AND FACT IN HISTORY

§ 1. *Introductory*

We described history, early in Chapter 2, as a significant narrative of human actions and experiences in the past. We have done something to elucidate and defend the first two parts of this description, and must now turn to the third, asking in what sense the historian's claim to reconstruct the past is justified. This will involve us immediately in the problem of historical truth, and ultimately in that of historical objectivity; and these will accordingly form the subjects of our next two chapters. As we shall see, the two subjects are closely connected, and might, indeed, be regarded as different aspects of a single topic.

The problem of truth is not peculiar to history, or for that matter to any branch of learning. It is a general philosophical question to know to what extent any judgment, or proposition, or statement (choose what term you will), expresses the nature of reality or states fact. But we should be clear from the first what is being asked here. We are not concerned with the justification of particular statements of any kind—with how, for instance, we know it is true that Julius Caesar was murdered or that chimaeras are imaginary creatures. Questions of that sort have to be answered by recognised experts in the different subjects concerned, or by reference to particular experiences. The philosophical problem of truth arises on a different level. It is not doubts about the truth of particular judgments, but scepticism about whether human beings can ever reach truth or state fact precisely, that the philosopher has to face. And it is with this form of scepticism, so far as it concerns the special case of historical judgments, that we shall be concerned in the present discussion. We have to enquire into certain general difficulties about the historian's ability to do what he says he is doing, namely, reconstructing the past, and this enquiry will involve us in a critical examination both of what it is to be an historical fact and of the nature of historical evidence.

It would only be candid to point out here that there are philosophers today who deny that there is a real problem of truth of the kind just stated. The only genuine questions about truth, they say, are those arising out of enquiries into the grounds of particular statements, and these must all be answered departmentally. Philosophical scepticism, for these writers, so far from being the indispensable prelude to clear and critical thinking it was once thought to be, is a profitless chase after a will-o'-the-wisp from which any sensible person would wish to be free.

Those convinced of the correctness of this point of view may well find that the discussions of the present chapter have a somewhat outmoded air, though they will not necessarily be wholly out of sympathy with their conclusions. Whether they are, in fact, unilluminating as well as (perhaps) unfashionable I must leave the reader to judge. I would only remark in advance that while the point of view in question has certainly proved helpful in clearing up obstinate problems in more than one philosophical field, it is by no means self-evident that all the traditional questions of philosophy can be satisfactorily dealt with by its methods; and that the problem of truth is one over which the issue is, in my view, still in doubt.

§ 2. *Truth as correspondence and truth as coherence*

It will be convenient to begin with a sketch of two of the most widely held philosophical theories of truth, and some remarks on their respective merits and demerits. We shall consider these theories first without special reference to the sphere of history, leaving the question of their applicability to that sphere for separate consideration.

The first theory is one to which we all subscribe in words at least. A statement, we say, is true if it corresponds to the facts;

and, conversely, if it corresponds to the facts it is true. Truth and correspondence with fact thus seem to be interchangeable terms, and the theory simply consists in stressing their equivalence. Truth, its supporters say, *means* correspondence with fact, so that no statement which does not so correspond can be true.

Thus stated the Correspondence theory, as it is called, will seem to the unsophisticated mind little more than a truism. But difficulties begin when we try to probe its apparently innocent formula. A statement is true, we are told, if it corresponds with fact; but what is fact? Here common language is ready with an answer. The facts in any sphere, we should normally say, are what they are independently of the enquirer into it; in some sense they exist whether or not anybody thinks about them. They are what we describe as 'hard', 'stubborn', or, again, as 'given'. Facts so understood are commonly contrasted with theories, which cannot as such lay claim to any of these dignified adjectives, but must be content to be at best 'well-grounded' or 'securely based.' The proper function of a theory is to 'explain', 'do justice to' or 'cover' the facts, which thus form for it an indispensable frame of reference.

The reader will experience no difficulty in thinking of suitable examples of situations to which this analysis clearly applies. Thus that I have such-and-such visual experiences is fact. An oculist may form a theory about my powers of vision, and that theory may be true or false. Whether it is depends on whether it 'covers' or 'does justice to' my experiences, which are not themselves true or false, but simply occur. If it is suggested that the theory can be true even if it fails to answer to my experiences, I shall have no hesitation in denouncing the suggestion as empty talk. The oculist's diagnosis, I shall say, must explain the facts from which it starts; it is no good if it ignores them.

The Correspondence theory of truth may thus be said to have the merit of itself corresponding with fact, at a certain level of sophistication at least. But its difficulties are by no means cleared up. No doubt it is possible—and indeed indispensable—to draw for practical purposes a distinction between what we consider to be 'hard' fact and what we think of as 'mere' theory; but the theoretical basis of the distinction is not so clear. Theories, we are all apt to suppose, are things which exist in people's heads, whilst facts are there whether we like them or not. Theories take the form of judgments, or propositions asserted or denied, or, less technically, of spoken, written or implied statements; facts are the material about which statements are made or judgments formulated. But the question we have to face is how we are to get at these independent facts to which our theories must conform, and it is a question to which it is by no means easy to find an answer. For, when we come to think about it, our theories, which exist in the form of actual or possible statements, are themselves tested by referring to other statements. The oculist's account of the defects of my vision, for instance, has to conform to the statements I make in response to his questions. It is not the case that he can know the facts directly and frame his theory accordingly; he has to decide what the facts are by considering the answers I give.

Now it may be suggested that the plausibility of this argument depends solely on the peculiarity of the chosen example. No doubt it is true that an oculist cannot know the facts about my vision directly, because he cannot see with my eyes; but because facts are not always directly accessible, it does not follow that they are never so. Must I not at least be myself aware of the true facts of the case and know what I see and what I do not? The visual experiences which were equated above with the facts in our example are after all my experiences, and presumably everyone knows his own experiences directly.

Yet the position is even so not wholly clear. For, after all, when we say we test a theory by referring to experiences the phrase is used somewhat loosely. Experiences in themselves cannot be used to test theories; they have to be expressed, given conceptual form, raised to the level of judgment, before they can serve that purpose. But in this process of expression the actual experience from which we set out is inevitably transformed. It is transformed by being interpreted—by being brought into relation with previous experiences of the same kind and classified under general concepts. Only if an experience is so interpreted can it be described, and only if it is described, or at least consciously apprehended by the person who has it, can it be used to check a theory. An experience which was not described but merely enjoyed could not be known in the sense in which we require to know the facts to which our statements must correspond.

The implication of these remarks should not be misunderstood.

They are not meant to refute the proposition that there is a given or, as some philosophers prefer to call it, an 'immediate' element in knowledge. That there is, I should say, is obvious, and those writers who lay stress on this given element as the source of all factual truth are in the right. But we cannot proceed from that to equate the sphere of the given with the sphere of fact, and assume that the philosophical problem of truth is solved. For the difficulty remains of seizing the given as it is given, and this seems to be just what we cannot do. The precise feelings we enjoy, the individual perceptions we have, are transformed when we come to interpret them. Yet unless we do interpret them we cannot use them in elaborating the structure of knowledge.

It follows from this that the distinction between fact and theory on which supporters of the Correspondence theory rely is one which cannot be taken as absolute. The facts to which our theories are to be referred must themselves be given propositional form (or, if you like, take shape as actual or possible statements) if they are to fulfil that function. But this means that an account of truth in terms of correspondence with fact can at best be a partial one. The notion of fact must be further explored, and an alternative analysis of it must be given.

At this point we may conveniently pass to our second main theory, the Coherence theory of truth. Here an attempt is made to define truth as a relation not between statement and fact, but between one statement and another. A statement, it is maintained, is true if it can be shown to cohere, or fit in with, all other statements we are prepared to accept. No actual statement we make, it is argued, is made entirely in isolation: they all depend on certain presuppositions or conditions, and are made against a background of these. Again, every belief we have is bound up with other beliefs, in the sense that it is part or the whole of our ground for accepting them, or they part or the whole of our ground for accepting it. The separate bits of our knowledge, in fact, form part of a system and, however little we realise it, the whole system is implicit in the assertion of any part of it. And the central contention of the theory we are examining is that it is on the systematic character of our knowledge that we must focus attention if we are to give a satisfactory account of truth.

Before making any comment on the theory, it will be well to

try to illustrate it in an example. Let us take the assertion that tomorrow will be wet and stormy, and consider how it would be treated by supporters of the Coherence theory. In the first place, they would point out that the assertion involves acceptance of a whole range of concepts and principles which are not peculiar to it, but which govern all statements and beliefs of the same kind: the concepts and principles which are set out in systematic form in the science of meteorology. And secondly, they would argue that the belief is not one which we form in isolation: we come to the conclusion that tomorrow will be wet and stormy because we have already committed ourselves to certain other assertions, such as that there is high cirrus cloud in the sky, that the sunset today has a certain appearance, and so on. Accordingly it is said that we cannot discuss the truth of the judgment from which we set out as if it were complete in itself, but must consider it as part of a whole system of judgments. Like an iceberg, the system is only partly visible, but it is none the less indubitably there.

It should be noticed that the Coherence theory does not dispense with the notion of fact, but offers a fresh interpretation of it. A fact for it is not something which exists whether or not anybody takes any notice of it; it is rather the conclusion of a process of thinking. Facts cannot, as was imagined in the Correspondence account, be simply apprehended: they have to be *established*. And this means that there is really no distinction of principle between a fact and a theory. A fact is simply a theory which has established itself, a theory about whose reliability serious doubts no longer exist. The support of common language, it may be remarked, can be claimed for this usage: it is sometimes said of evolution, for instance, that it is no longer theory, but fact.

It is true that acceptance of this interpretation involves us in the at first sight paradoxical assertion that the facts in any subject are only provisonally fixed, and are everywhere liable to be revised; but, provided we take care not to confuse this with the very different view that all beliefs are equally doubtful, there is no reason why we should not agree to it. The whole history of science, after all, goes to show that what is considered fact in one age is repudiated in another, and indeed it is hard to see how the different branches of learning could have made the progress they have if the matter were different. The alternative notion of scientific advance, formulated by Aristotle, who thought the edifice of knowledge would take final form from the first and would merely grow in bulk without alteration in structure, is now everywhere discredited.

So much by way of summary account of the theory. Of the many objections brought against it, it may be said at once that some spring from what might well be thought the extravagances of its supporters. Thus they tried to make out that the theory applied to all possible judgments or statements, and this involved them in difficulties both about mathematical and logical truths (which do not appear to be subject to revision in the same way as factual truths), and, still more obviously, about their own statement of the theory. If no statement can be pronounced finally true, what are we to say of the statement that truth is coherence? Again, in the interest of the monistic metaphysics they favoured, they argued that all truths formed part of a single system, which must accordingly be presupposed in all correct assertions. This had the appearance at least of suggesting that every fact must have direct bearing on every other fact—that, for instance, the weather in Australia today must have a bearing on what I eat for my tea in Oxford—when ordinary experience would suggest that it is utterly irrelevant. But it seems possible to accept the theory as giving a correct account of factual truths without committing ourselves to any such absurdities. Whatever view we take of the truth of mathematical and philosophical propositions, truths of fact may still be correctly explained by the Coherence theory. Nor is the contention that no judgment can be true in isolation, but all must be taken as falling within a system, overthrown by doubts about whether we can find a *single* system within which they all fall. The Coherence theory can be substantially correct, even if it cannot be used to support a monistic metaphysics.

Nevertheless, it must be admitted that the theory does wear an air of paradox. If it merely argued that coherence is to be taken as the *test* of truth it might be acceptable enough, for it is, in fact, the case that our various beliefs do fall into recognisable systems; but in *identifying* truth with coherence it appears to involve a fatal omission. What it omits is any reference to the element of independence which we associate with truth. We all believe that there is a distinction between truth, which holds whether we like it or not, and fiction, which we make up to suit ourselves. But if facts are to be pronounced the products of our thinking it looks as if we ought to be able to make them up too, and thus the distinction is blurred. Of course, supporters of the Coherence theory are perfectly aware of this objection, and are anxious to repudiate it. The thinking which leads to the establishment of fact, they say,[1] must not be supposed arbitrary: truth is attained only so far as I suppress my private self and allow my thinking to be guided by objective principles, universally valid. But the impression remains that the given element in experience is not satisfactorily accounted for by the theory, and that the 'hardness' of fact, a feature we all recognise in our unphilosophical moments, disappears if it is accepted.

We may sum up by saying that, whilst each of these standard theories of truth has its attractive features, neither is wholly free from difficulties. A fully (or more) satisfactory account would, it seems, have to embody points drawn from both. But instead of asking here whether any genuine synthesis of the two theories is possible, we must turn back to the special problem which concerns us in this chapter, and consider the nature of truth and fact in history.

§ 3. *History and the Correspondence theory*

The support of history has been claimed for both of the theories we have analysed, in each case with some plausibility.

Thus it is pointed out by supporters of the Correspondence view[2] that in history, if anywhere, we are concerned with facts which are fixed and determined just because they are past, facts which cannot by any stretch of imagination be thought to depend on what we are thinking now. History in the sense of the record of past events must correspond to history in the sense of *res gestae*; if it does not we shall have no hesitation in denouncing it as a fraud. Scientific truths can perhaps be accommodated to the requirements of the Coherence theory, because of the element of convention which scientific thinking undoubtedly includes; but historical truths cannot, for the facts with which history deals have actually occurred,

1. See, for instance, part III of H. H. Joachim's *Logical Studies*. Joachim's earlier book, *The Nature of Truth*, is perhaps the clearest exposition of the Coherence theory in English. The theory goes back to Hegel, who produced the well-known dictum that 'the truth is the whole'.
2. cf. A. M. MacIver, 'Historical Explanation,' reprinted in *Logic and Language*, second series, Ed. A. Flew, for some of these arguments.

and nothing we say or think about them now is going to alter them.

All this is convincing enough, yet there is a strong case on the other side too. The point on which the Coherence theory is chiefly insistent, that all truths are relative, is illustrated with particular clarity in the field of history. It can be argued with some effect that although the historian thinks he is talking about a past which is over and done with, everything he actually believes about that past is a function of the evidence at present available to him and of his own skill in interpreting it. The facts he recognises—which after all are the only facts he knows—are established in the way described in the Coherence theory; they do represent conclusions arrived at after processes of thinking, conclusions which incidentally are so far systematically related that an alteration in one can have a profound effect on all the rest. And if it is suggested that this cannot be all that the historian means when he speaks of fact, that he is thinking of the actual past and not merely our present reconstruction of it, of what, in fact, happened rather than of what we believe about it now, the reply will come that this something further can be shown to be in the last analysis chimerical. For facts which bear no relation to present evidence must be unknowable, and how they could have any significance in those circumstances, whether for historians or anyone else, is not apparent.[1]

It is clear enough that the real point at issue between the theories turns on the accessibility of the past to later knowledge. The Correspondence theory stakes everything on the notion of a past which is at once over and done with and capable of being reconstructed in some degree at least. Supporters of the Coherence view, by way of contrast, say that the two requirements cannot both be fulfilled, and argue that we must choose between a past which is independent and one which can be known.

Let us try to advance towards a solution by examining the Correspondence account in some detail. It can be put forward with varying degrees of sophistication. In all its forms it may be said to liken the historian's task to the construction of a mosaic. The past, it argues, consisted of a series of separate events, and it is the historian's job to reconstruct the series, or a part of it, as fully as he

1. A good statement of the Coherence theory as applied to history is to be found in Michael Oakeshott's *Experience and its Modes*, ch. III.

can. If now it is asked how the job is done, the simplest answer is that some events were recorded as they occurred, and that all we have to do is read the records. Ancient historians who wrote of contemporary events, like Thucydides and Caesar, military and civil governors setting up tablets to commemorate their deeds, medieval chroniclers and modern diarists may be mentioned as instances of persons who recorded events as they actually happened (or perhaps a little later), and whose records can accordingly be taken as providing a basis of hard fact round which the historian can build the rest of his narrative. Historical truth, on this account, depends on our accepting certain primary authorities, at least some of whose statements are treated as wholly authentic.

That this notion of authorities has an important part to play in historical thinking I should not wish to deny. Yet to suggest that any historian who knows his job would be ready to accept a statement as true just because it is recorded by such an authority is surely absurd. No doubt there are occasions on which our only evidence for a past event is a record of that sort; but that illustrates not the extent of the historian's trust in primary sources, but rather the poverty of the material with which he works. The simple consideration that our confidence in even the best authorities is increased by the discovery of independent evidence for what they say is enough to expose the hollowness of the authority theory. And the truth is that it belongs to a stage of historical thinking which is now outmoded. Dependence on the *ipse dixit* of an authority seemed natural enough in the early days of historiography, or again in those ages when appeal to authority was normal in every sphere. But whatever part faith may have to play elsewhere, it is entirely out of place in developed historical thinking. A modern historian's attitude to his authorities must be everywhere critical: he must submit all his evidence, with whatever authority it comes, to the same sceptical scrutiny, building his facts out of it rather than taking it for fact without further ado.

Appeal to authority will thus not serve as a ground for a correspondence theory of historical truth. But the last sentence of the preceding paragraph may suggest an alternative account. Every working historian, it can be argued, draws a distinction between the conclusions to which he comes, the picture of the past he finally builds up, and the material from which he sets out, which exists in the shape of historical evidence—documents, coins, remains of buildings, and so on. He may regard his conclusions as provisional only, but he cannot take up the same attitude towards his evidence. Unless this is taken as firm and beyond doubt, as an ultimate which is not to be questioned, there can be no progress on the road to historical truth.

Here again we are dealing with a theory which corresponds closely to common-sense ideas and for that very reason undoubtedly contains much that is attractive. Yet it owes some of its attraction to an important ambiguity. When we say that every historian believes that there is evidence for the past, and that this evidence is something he will not presume to doubt, what do we mean? If it is only that there exist now certain documents, buildings, coins, etc., which are believed to date from this period or that, the statement is not likely to be questioned. It is no part of the historian's task to doubt the evidence of his senses: he takes that for granted just as natural scientists do. But the case is altered if we understand the statement in a different (and perfectly natural) sense. If it is taken to mean that there is a fixed body of historical evidence, whose implications are plain for all to see, serious doubts arise about it. They do so in the first place because of the consideration, obvious enough to anyone with first-hand experience of historical work, that historians must not only decide to what conclusions their evidence points, but further what they are to recognise as evidence. In a sense, of course, everything in the physical world now is evidence for the past, and much of it for the human past. But it is not all equally evidence for any given series of past events, and it sets the historian a problem just because of that. The problem is that of excluding bogus and admitting only genuine evidence for the events under review, and it is a most important part of historical work that it should be properly solved.

And there is another point which needs to be emphasised. The suggestion that there is evidence for the past is easily confused with the different suggestion that there are propositions about the past which we can affirm with certainty, and the confusion is particularly important if we are discussing the merits of the Correspondence theory. For supporters of that theory, as we have seen, must, if they are to make out their case, point to some body of knowledge (in the strict sense of that term in which what we know is beyond question) by which to test our beliefs, and their recourse to historical evidence in the case we are examining was undertaken precisely with that purpose in mind. But it should not be very difficult to see that to read them in that way and make them say that historical evidence gives us so much knowledge about the past is in effect to revive the authority theory. The only difference is that instead of pinning our faith to written texts we now base ourselves on historical evidence generally, including archaeological and numismatic as well as literary and epigraphic data. But the procedure is no more plausible in the one case than in the other, for it remains true that evidence of all kinds needs interpretation, and the very fact that it does means that no statement about the past can be true in isolation.

The truth is, I think, that we can believe that there is good evidence for the past without believing that *any* propositions about it are beyond question. If the Correspondence theory were to assert that and nothing more, then we should have no cause to quarrel with it. But it is seldom formulated, and perhaps cannot be satisfactorily formulated, in that very modest way. The normal procedure of those who identify truth with correspondence, in the sphere of history as in that of perception, is to look for basic statements of fact which cannot be questioned, fundamental propositions which we can be said to know beyond possibility of correction. But the search is no more successful in history than it is elsewhere. The basic propositions to which we point—'here is a coin struck by Vespasian', 'this is a college account book dated 1752', might be examples—all embody an element of interpretation as well as something given. So-called 'atomic' propositions, which 'picture' fact precisely, are simply not to be found, in the sphere of history at least.

It may be objected to this that it ignores the special case, all-important for the historian, of memory knowledge. It has been argued, indeed,[1] that the historical past cannot be identified with the remembered past, and this would seem to be clear enough from the consideration that we hope as historians to go far beyond the range of living memory in our reconstruction of past events. Memory knowledge is by no means always, or perhaps even often, among the explicit data from which historians argue. But this does not alter the fact that historical thinking depends on memory in a

1. cf. Oakeshott, op. cit., p. 102.

quite special way. If there were no such thing as memory, it is doubtful if the notion of the past would make sense for us at all. And the argument we have to face here is just that memory, sometimes at least, gives us direct contact with the past, enabling us to make statements about it which are in principle beyond doubt. Memory, it is said, must be a form of knowledge in the strict sense: the very fact that we condemn some memories as unreliable shows as much. Part of the evidence for the judgment that memory is liable to mislead consists of memories of occasions on which we have ourselves been misled by it, and unless these memories are treated as authentic the wider judgment could never be made.

It is scarcely possible in the present context to discuss the problem of memory in the detail which it deserves, or even to indicate the reservations with which the above theory must be put forward. All we can do is make a single general point about it, a point which, however, seems fatal to the objection we are considering. It is that it is impossible to separate the pure deliverances of memory from the constructions we ourselves put upon them. When we say we remember something now, does our memory give us an exact and unaltered picture of an event which happened in the past? No doubt we often think it does, and no doubt our assumption is a valid one for practical purposes. But when we reflect that we are forced to look at the past through the eyes of the present and accommodate what we see to the conceptual scheme we use now, our confidence is shaken, and we begin to realise that what may be called pure memory, in which we deal only with what is given in experience, and memory judgment, in which we seek to interpret the given, are stages distinguishable in principle but not in practice. And once we recognise this we find the claim that some memory statements are pure transcriptions of fact very difficult to sustain.

The case of memory, here again, appears to be precisely parallel to that of sense-perception. Supporters of the Correspondence theory of truth have often tried to argue that sense-perception gives us direct knowledge of the real world, and is as such a source of incorrigible truths of fact. But the argument breaks down once we draw the important distinction between sensation and sense-perception proper. Sensation, no doubt, gives us immediate contact with the real, but it is to sense-perception that we must advance if we are to say anything about the experience, and the judgments of sense-perception in the strict sense are certainly not incorrigible. Similarly with memory knowledge. Pure memory, as I have called it, gives us immediate access to the past, but it does not follow that we grasp the past precisely as it was in memory, knowing it as it were by a species of pure intuition. The truth would seem rather to be that we have a basis on which to reconstruct it, but no means of looking at it face to face.

§ 4. *History and the Coherence theory*

The reader will observe that throughout this discussion of the Correspondence theory as applied to history we have made use of criticisms drawn from the stock-in-trade of its rival. And he may well be curious to know whether this means that we ourselves accept the Coherence theory as correct in this sphere, and if so how we propose to deal with the paradoxes it seems to involve.

I am not anxious to undertake a further extensive survey and critique, more especially as the outlines of a Coherence view of historical truth have been suggested in the foregoing pages, and shall ask leave to consider only one or two of the more pressing difficulties in such a view.

We may put the argument against a Coherence theory of truth in history on some such lines as the following. According to the Coherence theory, as we saw, all truth is essentially relative: it depends, in the first place, upon the presuppositions and conceptual scheme with which we set out, in the second on the rest of our beliefs in the field in question. But, we shall be told, this theory, if honestly applied, would effectively prevent our ever building up a body of historical truth. Unless he can affirm that there are some facts which he knows for certain, there is nothing for the historian to build on. All knowledge must begin from a basis which is taken as unquestioned, and all factual knowledge from a basis in fact. The alternative, the relativism of the Coherence theory, leaves the whole structure in the air, with the result that we have no effective criterion for distinguishing between the real and the imaginary. Coherence, in short, is not enough as an account of historical truth: we need to be assured of contact with reality as well. And it may be added that a glance at actual historical procedure bears these contentions out. For historians do certainly recognise some facts as established beyond question—that Queen Victoria came to the throne in 1837 and died in 1901, for instance—and it is on the basis of these that they build up their whole account.

There are two main points in this criticism, one of which appears to the present writer very much more effective than the other. The first is the simple assertion that the historian does regard some of his facts as certain and that this cannot be reconciled with the Coherence theory. But why should it not? What the Coherence theory maintains, in effect, is that all historical judgments are, strictly speaking, probable only every one is in principle subject to revision as knowledge accumulates. But it is perfectly possible to take up this position without assigning the *same* degree of probability to every historical statement. Supporters of the Coherence theory of historical truth are not precluded from accepting some judgments as better established, even incomparably better established, than others: like the rest of us, they can be very confident about one, fairly well convinced of a second, and highly doubtful of a third. The one thing they cannot say is that any judgment is so secure that it cannot be shaken even in principle. But no one who knows anything about the actual course of historical thought would want them to make such a claim.

This may seem a paradox, yet the position is, I think, really quite clear. It can be illustrated by comparing the historian's procedure with that of the detective, a favourite analogy of Collingwood's which is very much to the point here. A detective investigating a case begins by deciding what he can regard as undisputed fact, in order to build his theories around that as a framework. If the theories work out, the framework will be declared to have been well-founded, and no further questions will be asked about it. But if results are not forthcoming, a stage may be reached at which it is necessary to go back to the beginning and doubt some of the initial 'facts' of the case. A detective who, through devotion to the Correspondence theory of truth, refused to take that step would be very little use in his profession, though naturally he would not be encouraged to take it till every other expedient failed. The case of the historian is exactly parallel. He also must be prepared, if necessary, to doubt even his firmest beliefs—even, for example, the chronological framework inside which he arranges his results[1]—though it does not follow that he will involve himself in such an

1. As has, in fact, been done more than once for the history of ancient Egypt.

upheaval lightly. He will indeed do all he can to avoid it, undertaking it only as a last resort, but all the same he must not rule it out in principle.

The point about our confidence in the certainty of some historical facts is thus not fatal to the Coherence theory, since it is practical, not mathematical, certainty which is there in question. As Hume saw, we do distinguish in the sphere of matter of fact between what we consider to be 'proved' and what we regard as 'merely' probable. But the distinction, as he might have added, is in the end a relative one, since the contrary of every matter-of-fact statement, even one about which we are supremely confident, is always logically possible. No such statement, whether in history or elsewhere, can be raised to the status of a logically necessary truth.

The other main charge in the criticism of the Coherence theory of historical truth outlined above is, however, a different matter. It is that an account of historical truth in terms of coherence only leaves the whole structure of historical beliefs in the air, without any necessary connection with reality. Not unnaturally this position is readily identified with one of complete scepticism about historical knowledge, and we must clearly examine it with some care.

Let us investigate the charge by considering the account of truth and fact in history given by a well-known supporter of the Coherence theory who has also been a professional historian, Professor Michael Oakeshott. In his book, *Experience and its Modes*,[1] Professor Oakeshott agrees that the historian 'is accustomed to think of the past as a complete and virgin world stretching out behind the present, fixed, finished and independent, awaiting only discovery' (p. 106). 'It is difficult,' he adds (p. 107), 'to see how he could go on did he not believe his task to be the resurrection of what once had been alive.' But for all that the belief is an absurdity.

A fixed and finished past, a past divorced from and uninfluenced by the present, is a past divorced from evidence (for evidence is always present) and is consequently nothing and unknowable. The fact is ... that the past in history varies with the present, rests upon the present, is the present. 'What really happened' ... must, if history is to be rescued from nonentity, be replaced by 'what the evidence obliges us to believe.' ... There are

1. Originally published in 1933 and reissued in 1967. cf. also p. 192 below.

not two worlds—the world of past happenings and the world of our present knowledge of those past events—there is only one world, and it is a world of present experience.[1]

Indeed, it is because the historian in the end refuses to recognise the full implications of this statement—because he obstinately clings to the notion of an independent past and retains an element of correspondence in his working theory of truth—that Professor Oakeshott finally condemns historical thinking as not fully rational, but a 'mode' or 'arrest' of experience only.

Here we have the main paradox of the Coherence theory of historical truth set forth in all its nakedness. It is the paradox expressed in the well-known dictum of Croce's, that all history is contemporary history, and I suggest that it is one which no working historian can be got to accept. Professor Oakeshott, it should be remarked, is himself aware of this: he distinguishes, in the passage from which I have quoted, between the past as it is *for* history and the past as it is *in* history, the former being the past as viewed by the historian, the latter the past as philosophically interpreted. Having the courage of his convictions, he proceeds to set the past *for* history aside, saying that the common notion of it is a simple misconception of the character of the past *of* or *in* history.

But it may be questioned, in the first place, whether this apparently high-handed procedure, which tells the historian that his beliefs are nonsense because they will not fit the results of a previously formulated philosophical position, is a sound one. And even if it can be defended (and some philosophers would certainly regard it as defensible), there appears to be a fatal ambiguity in Oakeshott's argument.[2]

When it is said that our knowledge of the past must rest on evidence which is present that is one thing; but when the conclusion is drawn that the past *is* the present, that is quite another. Evidence for the past must no doubt be present in the sense of being presented to us now, but it does not follow from this that it must *refer to* present time, as it would have to if Oakeshott's conclusion were to be justified. And indeed it is a characteristic of the evidence with which historians deal that it refers not to the present, but the

1. op cit., pp. 107–8.
2. Compare G. C. Field, *Some Problems of the Philosophy of History* (British Academy lecture, 1938), pp. 15–16.

past. It is rooted in the past just because of the close connection between history and memory we noted above. As we saw, memory cannot be said to make us directly acquainted with past fact, but it does for all that give us access to the past. Reference to the past, involving the assertion of the proposition 'something happened', is an essential part of remembering, just as reference to an external world, involving the assertion of the proposition 'there are external objects or events', is an essential part of perception. Different philosophers have very different analyses to offer of these propositions; but the one thing which would not seem to be open to them is to explain them away altogether.

We may conclude that the Coherence theory, at least in its normal form, will not apply to history. But as we have previously criticised various attempts to state a Correspondence theory of historical truth, we must clearly ask where we stand. The answer, I suggest, is that we have been attempting a synthesis of the two views. Whilst denying the proposition that historians know any absolutely certain facts about the past and arguing with the Coherence party that all historical statements are relative, we nevertheless agree with supporters of the Correspondence view in asserting that there is an attempt in history, as in perception, to characterise an independent reality. And we should maintain that the assertion is not gratuitous because historical judgment, whatever its superstructure, has its foundation in a peculiar sort of experience, a kind of experience in which we have access to the past though no direct vision of it. There is in fact a given element in historical thinking, even though that element cannot be isolated. We cannot carry out the full programme of the Correspondence theory because we cannot examine the past to see what it was like; but our recon-struction of it is not therefore arbitrary. Historical thinking is controlled by the need to do justice to the evidence, and while that is not fixed in the way some would have us believe, it is none the less not made up by the historian. There is something 'hard' about it, something which cannot be argued away, but must simply be accepted. And it is doubtless this element which leads supporters of the Correspondence theory to try to find the criterion of historical truth in the conformity of statements to independently known facts. The project is one which is bound to fail, yet there remains a standing temptation to make it.

§ 5. *Criticisms of the intermediate position*

Our attempted synthesis will doubtless come under attack from both sides: we may expect to be told on the one hand that it depends on nothing more than unproved assertion, on the other that it offers too flimsy a barrier to the inroads of historical scepticism. To the first criticism we might reply that if we are making an assumption it is one which all historians, and for that matter all sensible persons, share. In any case, what more can be offered? Are we required to *prove* that there were past events? Some critics may suggest that we are if our account is to be fully defensible, but we may well wonder whether they have not got themselves into a state where they cannot be satisfied. Our experience is such that we classify events as past, present or future, just as it is such that we classify them as happening in the external world or in ourselves, and we can no more be expected to prove that there were past events than that we experience an external world. Memory is our sole guarantee of the one just as our possession of external senses is our sole guarantee of the other. This does not mean that philosophical attempts to *analyse* such notions as those of the past and the external world are, as some modern philosophers suggest, futile; on the contrary, such analyses can be genuinely illuminating. But it does mean that any effort to deduce them, by finding for them a logically necessary foundation, must end in failure.

To the second criticism that we offer too feeble a defence against historical scepticism we can retort only by reiterating our previous arguments against those theories which try to put forward something more substantial. In the course of the present chapter we have examined several attempts to find for the historian a set of unshakable facts to serve as a basis for his knowledge, but in every case we found the account open to criticism. Of other theories which proceed on the same general lines, we may mention the views of Dilthey and Collingwood, discussed in Chapter 3. But we saw (p. 51) above that Dilthey's account did not avoid the general difficulties of a representative theory of knowledge, whilst Collingwood's, though expressly designed to do just that, was able to achieve its object only by making use of a most questionable expedient. It may be useful to try to show what this was.

In a very difficult section in his *Idea of History* (part V, section 4, pp. 282 ff.) Collingwood argued that there was a sense in which a past act of thinking, whether my own or someone's else, could be revived by me now, though not with precisely the same background as it originally had. He based his case on the consideration that acts of thought are not mere constituents of the temporal flow of consciousness, but things which can be sustained over a stretch of time and revived after an interval. A proposition of Euclid, for instance, can be contemplated by me for several seconds together, or again can be brought before my mind after my attention has wandered from it, and if I ask how many acts of thinking are involved in the one case or the other, the proper answer, Collingwood held, for each is one only. But if this holds of my own acts of thinking, it should hold also of cases where I am dealing with other people's thoughts: those of Julius Caesar, for instance. Here too the same act of thinking is in principle capable of being revived, though the background of feeling and emotion against which it was originally thought is not. And because this is so knowledge of the past is a real possibility: there is something about the past, namely certain past acts of thinking, which we can really grasp, though the process of doing so is one whose difficulties Collingwood had no wish to write down.

The argument, as always with Collingwood, is marked by great ingenuity. But an objection to it readily occurs: that the required identity is to be found in the *content* of what is thought rather than in the *act* of thinking itself. If this is right, I may think the same thought, in the sense of the same thought-content, as Julius Caesar, but not revive his precise act of thinking. The objection was anticipated by Collingwood (op. cit., p. 288) and rejected on the ground that if I could only think the same thought-content as Caesar and not revive his act of thinking, I could never know that my thoughts were identical with his. But there appear to be important ambiguities in this position. In one sense of the word 'thought', that in which it is taken to mean act or process of thinking, my thoughts can never be identical with anyone else's: saying they are mine indicates as much. Yet in another sense, where 'thought' is equated with what a man thinks, two persons can certainly think the same thoughts, and, what is more, can know that they do. But they know it not because their acts of thinking are identical (how could they be?), but because they find they can understand each other. Misled like so many others by the fatal word 'know', Collingwood has put forward an impossible solution for a difficulty which is perhaps not real at all.

It looks from this as if we must try to find a basis for historical knowledge not in our possession of a number of hard-and-fast past facts, but, more vaguely, in the given element in historical evidence. As I have tried to show, memory gives us access to the past, but not a direct vision of it. Thus all we can claim is to have a point of contact with past events, enabling us perhaps to divine their true shape in some degree, but not such that we can check our reconstructions by comparing them with it to see how far they are correct. For the rest, the sole criterion of truth available to us, in history as in other branches of factual knowledge, is the internal coherence of the beliefs we erect on that foundation.

5

CAN HISTORY BE OBJECTIVE?

§ 1. *Importance of the notion of objectivity in history*

Despite the length of the foregoing discussions, we cannot claim to have done more than scratch the surface of the problem of historical truth. For though we have argued (or perhaps only asserted) that truth about the past is in principle attainable by the historian, we have so far said nothing of the many difficulties which might be expected to prevent his attaining it in practice. To discuss these difficulties we must pass on to what seems to the present writer at once the most important and the most baffling topic in critical philosophy of history, the problem of historical objectivity.

It may perhaps be helpful if I try to show why I think this problem is of central importance for philosophy of history. To do so will involve a somewhat devious approach and, I fear, a good deal of repetition of what has already been said. But perhaps that will be pardoned if it serves to make a crucial point clear.

Our main concern in the preceding chapters of this book has been to examine the nature of historical thinking and determine the status of history *vis-à-vis* other branches of learning and types of human activity; in particular we have been occupied with the question of its relations to the natural sciences. The problem is forced on us from two sides at once. On the one hand we have the claims made by positivistically-minded philosophers that these sciences are the sole repositories of human knowledge, a claim which, if accepted, would make history something other than a cognitive activity; on the other we have the suggestion, put forward by certain idealist philosophers who have themselves (as the positivists mostly have not) first-hand experience of historical work, that history is entitled to rank alongside, if not above, the natural sciences: that it is an autonomous branch of learning, with a subject-matter and methods of its own, resulting in a type of knowledge which is not reducible to any other. The two positions stand sharply opposed to one another, and the need to examine them is all the more urgent when we take note of the assertion sometimes made (for example, by Collingwood) that the emergence of history as an autonomous discipline is the distinctive feature of the intellectual life of the present age. If this claim has any substance it is clear that philosophers who continue to ignore history are conspicuously failing to do their job.

Now on the whole the results of our previous discussions commit us to sympathy with the idealist rather than the positivist view of the status of history. We suggested in Chapter 2 that history is rather co-ordinate with natural science than with simple perception, and in Chapter 3 we saw reason to reject the equation of historical thinking with the thinking of common sense. In the same chapter we argued that historical explanation involves certain features which appear to be peculiar to itself. We did indeed reject the claim that historians are able to attain concrete knowledge of particular facts by the exercise of some unique form of intuitive apprehension: to define history, as has sometimes been done, as the 'science of the individual', seemed to be either uninteresting or indefensible. But though we stressed the operation in historical thinking of generalisations borrowed from other disciplines and for the most part not made explicit by the historian, we remained none the less disposed to accept the view that history *is* an autonomous branch of learning and thus a kind of science in its own right.

But before we can finally commit ourselves to the assertion that history is a genuine science, in the wider meaning of that term, we must face a difficulty which was referred to earlier but there put aside. It is the difficulty of whether, and in what sense, historians can hope to attain objective knowledge.

In a previous chapter (pp. 36–7 above) it was pointed out that objectivity is one of the characteristics which, according to common belief, must be present in any knowledge which can claim scientific status. And by describing a body of propositions as 'objective' in this context we mean that they are such as to warrant acceptance by all who seriously investigate them. Thus we describe the results of a particular piece of work in physics as making a contribution to objective knowledge when we think that *any* competent physicist who repeated the work would reach those results. The point of the description is to emphasise the universal character of scientific thinking: the fact that it is impartial and impersonal, and in consequence communicable to others and capable of repetition. That thinking in the natural sciences has achieved this sort of objectivity to a high degree, so that we can normally expect that two or more competent scientists who started with the same evidence would achieve the same results, is a strikingly obvious fact. What has made it possible is another matter.

I can scarcely undertake a detailed discussion of the concept of objectivity in the natural sciences here, and can therefore only suggest dogmatically that the basis of it is to be found, not so much in the fact that those sciences are concerned with an independent object, the physical world, but rather in that each of them has evolved a standard way of thinking about its subject-matter. At any stage of the development of a science, the exponents of that science are more or less agreed on the leading assumptions they are to make about their material and the leading principles they are to adopt in dealing with it. The main presuppositions of the thinking of physics, for example, are shared by all physicists, and to think scientifically about physical questions is to think in accordance with them. And this is at any rate one of the things which gives general validity to the conclusions of physicists: they do not depend in any important sense on the personal idiosyncrasies or private feelings of those who reach them, but are reached by a process in which complete abstraction is made from these.

These remarks should not be misunderstood. In speaking of the natural sciences having each evolved a standard way of thinking about its subject-matter I must not be taken to imply that each of them has one fundamental, unchanging set of presuppositions which all who work at the subject can clearly see. Any such suggestion would conflict with the obvious facts that the principles of a science are only imperfectly grasped by those who pursue it, and that they are themselves liable to be dropped or at any rate developed in the course of time. The proper interpretation of these changes is a most interesting question, but we cannot go into it here. Nor is it necessary to do so. For the purpose of assessing the status of the propositions of history it is enough to notice that the standard ways of thinking in the natural sciences of which we have spoken are generally recognised at any particular time, with the result that arguments and conclusions in those sciences can claim general acceptance in the scientific world. Natural science provides objective knowledge in this important sense. The question we have to face is whether the same can be said of history.

What I want to suggest (though this may be thought to beg the question at the outset) is that if history is to be pronounced a science in any sense of the term there must be found in it some feature answering to the objectivity of the natural sciences. Historical objectivity may not be of exactly the same species as scientific, yet it would surely be extremely paradoxical if the two had nothing in common. In particular, we may expect the natural scientific ideal of impartiality to be reflected in historical thinking if that thinking is to be shown to be philosophically respectable. If it is not—if historical interpretations can be said to hold only for this individual or that, or even for this class of individuals or that—then popular thought at least is likely to boggle at the description of history as a genuine science. And philosophers will certainly have cause to sympathise with popular thought here, since the notion of truth itself seems to involve indifference to persons or places, though not, in the case of factual truths, indifference to the evidence on the basis of which they are reached.

§ 2. *Preliminary statement of the problem*

With these considerations in mind, let us now turn to history itself and ask what the position there is. Do historians aim at objectivity in anything like the scientific sense? Is it their hope to produce results which any enquirer who started from the same evidence might be expected to accept?

It is not easy to give a straightforward answer to these questions, for the facts are not simple. Certainly it is true that reputable historians are united in demanding a species of impartiality and impersonality in historical work: historical writing in which arguments and conclusions are twisted to suit the personal prejudices or propagandist aims of the writer is universally condemned as bad. Whatever it is, genuine history is thought by historians to be distinguishable from propaganda, and would be said to have objective validity just because of that. But there is another side to the matter. One of the things which strikes the outsider most when he looks at history is the plurality of divergent accounts of the same subject which he finds. Not only is it true that each generation finds it necessary to rewrite the histories written by its predecessors; at any given point of time and place there are available differing and apparently inconsistent versions of the same set of events, each of them claiming to give, if not the whole truth about it, at any rate as much of the truth as can now be come by. The interpretations of one historian are indignantly repudiated by another, and how to reconcile them is not apparent, since the disputes are not merely technical (over the correct interpretation of evidence), but rather depend on ultimate preconceptions which in this case are emphatically not universally shared.

It appears from this that there functions in historical thinking a subjective element different from that which is to be found in scientific thinking, and that this factor limits, or alters the character of, the objectivity which historians can hope to attain. And it is important to notice that the suggestion is not one which historians would themselves necessarily repudiate. Whatever their predecessors fifty years ago may have thought, there seems no doubt that many historians today would feel uncomfortable if asked to free them-selves from all particular preconceptions and approach their facts in a wholly impersonal way. To aim at the impersonality of physics in history, they would say, is to produce something which is not history at all. And they could back up their assertion by arguing that every history is written from a certain point of view and makes sense only from that point of view. Take away all points of view, and you will have nothing intelligible left, any more than you will have anything visible if you are asked to look at a physical object, but not from any particular point of view.

This argument, which is, I believe, an important one, can be reinforced by further considerations. A concept which is extremely prominent in historical thinking is that of *selection*. History is selective in at least two senses. (*a*) Every actual piece of historical

D

writing is departmental, since it is only on an aspect or limited set of aspects of the past that a particular historian can concentrate his attention, and this remains true however wide the range of his interests. To construct a concrete picture of life as it was lived in the past may, as was asserted earlier, be the ideal of history, but if so it is an ideal to which no individual historian can make more than a limited contribution. And (*b*) no historian can narrate everything that happened in the past even within the field he chooses for study: all must select some facts for special emphasis and ignore others altogether. To put it very platitudinously, the only facts which find their way into history books are those which have some degree of importance. But the idea of what is important in history is doubly relative. It relates (*a*) to what happened independently of anyone's thinking now, but also (*b*) to the person making the judgment of importance. And in dealing with it we cannot eliminate the second factor altogether, as can be seen from the consideration that each historian obviously does bring to his studies a set of interests, beliefs and values which is clearly going to have some influence on what he takes to be important.

It would be easy enough at this stage to urge the conclusion that history is radically and viciously subjective, and in the light of that to write off its pretensions to be scientific in any sense of the term. But such a proceeding would be, I suggest, altogether too simple-minded. The notion of a 'point of view' in history, with which we have been working, is clearly in need of critical scrutiny, and it is difficult without an analysis of it to state any view on our subject satisfactorily. I propose, therefore, at this point to give the discussion a more concrete turn and ask what in particular it is that leads historians to disagree. This procedure should have the advantage of enabling us to put the question 'can history be objective?' in its true perspective, by distinguishing various levels at which it arises. For if anything is clear from the interminable popular discussions of prejudice in history it is that different sorts of subjective factor can enter into historical thinking, and that some of these constitute a far graver problem for philosophy of history than others. The survey which follows should at least preserve us from asking a portmanteau question, to which a simple answer is expected when none can be given.

§ 3. Factors making for disagreement among historians

I suggest that the main factors which actually make for disagreement among historians[1] may be grouped under the following four heads. First, personal likes and dislikes, whether for individuals or classes of person. Historian A (Carlyle would be an example) admires great men; historian B (e.g., Wells) has a strong antipathy to them. Historian A, in consequence, makes his whole narrative centre round the ideas and actions of his hero, which he presents as decisive for the history of the time; historian B goes out of his way to write down the same actions as (for example) muddled, insincere, vicious or ineffective. Secondly, prejudices or, to use a less colourful word, assumptions associated with the historian's membership of a certain group: the assumptions he makes, for example, as belonging to this or that nation, race or social class, or again as professing this or that religion. Thirdly, conflicting theories of historical interpretation. Historian A is a Marxist and sees the ultimate explanation of all historical events in the operation of economic factors; historian B (Bertrand Russell is an example) is a pluralist and refuses to regard any single type of causal factor as decisive in history. Whilst agreeing with some Marxist conclusions there are others which he cannot bring himself to accept. Fourthly, basically different moral beliefs, conceptions of the nature of man or, if the term is preferred, *Weltanschauungen*. The influence of this last group is perhaps most readily illustrated in the different results produced by those who approach history with a background of Christian beliefs and those whose approach is 'rationalist' in the eighteenth-century sense.

Without enquiring into the adequacy or exhaustiveness of this classification, I shall proceed at once to make some remarks on each of the four groups of factor, with a view to determining, if possible, which should claim our special attention in the present discussion.

(*a*) *Personal bias.* The position in regard to this is, I think, com-

---

1. I must make clear that the kind of disagreement with which I am concerned in what follows is not disagreement about what conclusions to draw from a given body of (often inadequate) evidence, but rather disagreement about the proper interpretation of the conclusions drawn. Disagreement of the first kind seems to me largely a technical matter, though I should add that, for reasons which will appear from Chapter 4, I should not accept the distinction between fact and interpretation as ultimately tenable.

paratively simple. There is, of course, plenty of evidence of the influence of personal likes and dislikes both in the judgments historians make and (more important) in their general presentation of facts, but it is doubtful, all the same, whether we should regard bias of this kind as a serious obstacle to the attainment of objective truth in history. It is doubtful for the simple reason that we all know from our own experience that this kind of bias can be corrected or at any rate allowed for. Once we recognise our own partialities, as we certainly can, we are already on our guard against them, and provided that we are sufficiently sceptical they need hold no further terrors for us. And we do hold that historians ought to be free from personal prejudice and condemn those historians who are not. It is a common reproach to Thucydides, for instance, that his dislike of Cleon led him to give an inaccurate account of the political history of his time. He could not help his feelings about the man, but they ought not to have been imported into his history. The same would be said, *mutatis mutandis*, about cases where the object of an historian's enthusiasm or aversion is a whole class of person—clerics, or scientists, or Germans, for example. Wells' antipathy to all notable military figures in his *Outline of History* is universally condemned as bad history on just these grounds.

(*b*) *Group prejudice*. In principle the same account must be given of the factors which fall under this heading as of those in our first class, though with certain important reservations. The reservations arise in the first place from the obvious fact that assumptions we make as members of a group are less easy to detect and therefore to correct than are our personal likes and dislikes. They are more subtle and widespread in their operation, and just because of their general acceptance in the group there is less urge for us to become conscious of them and so overcome them. Moreover, there is a difficulty about some of the factors in this class which is not found at all in the first. Our personal likes and dislikes rest primarily on our feelings, but it would be claimed that some of our group assumptions are of another character altogether: they have rational warrant, and so are not strictly matters of prejudice, but of principle. We should all say, for instance, that a man's religious opinions ought not to influence his history to the extent of making him incapable of doing justice to the actions of men who did not share them; but many would add that it would be absurd to require him to abstract from them altogether in what he writes. The case for that view would rest on the contention that, despite much facile assumption on the point, religious beliefs are not obviously the product of irrational prejudice only, but may be held as a matter of rational conviction. And if this is so it is not only inevitable but perfectly proper that they should exert an influence on the historian's thinking.

I do not wish to argue this particular case for its own sake, but only to make the general point. Its existence, however, should not jeopardise our main contention about this class of subjective factor, which we can put as follows. The assumptions which historians make as (for example) patriotic Englishmen, class-conscious members of the proletariat or staunch Protestants must be such as they can justify on rational grounds, or they must be extruded from their history. And we all believe the extrusion possible, in principle at least. To claim this is indeed to claim no more than that rational thinking is possible, that our opinions can be grounded as well as caused. It is true that the claim is one which would be dogmatically rejected in many quarters today: Marxists and Freudians, in their different ways, have taught us all to look for non-rational causes for ideas and beliefs which on the surface look perfectly rational, and have convinced some of us that rational thinking as such is an impossibility. But though we cannot (and should not) return to the naïve confidence of our grandfathers in these matters, it must none the less be pointed out that the anti-rationalist case here cannot be stated without contradiction. It undermines not only the theories of which its proponents disapprove, but itself as well. For it asks us to believe, as a matter of rational conviction, that rational conviction is impossible. And this we cannot do.[1]

(c) *Conflicting theories of historical interpretation.* By a theory of historical interpretation I mean a theory of the relative importance of different kinds of causal factor in history. It is plain enough that historians do employ such theories even when they do not explicitly formulate them, and again that there is no agreement among them about which of the many possible theories of this

---

1. Others who ask us to commit the same fallacy include the Behaviourist psychologists and certain modern sociologists (e.g. Mannheim). For a trenchant criticism of the latter see Dr. Popper's *Open Society*, ch. XXIII (vol. II, pp. 200 ff.).

kind is correct. Conflicting theories of historical interpretation are thus an important source of historical disagreement. And at first sight at least they present a more serious problem than the two classes of subjective factor we have so far considered. We have argued that historians can, if they make the effort, overcome the effects of personal bias and group prejudice. But we cannot urge the same solution of the difficulties which now confront us, by telling the historian to dispense with any theory of historical interpretation. For some such theory he must have, if he is to make any sense of his facts.

We may well be told at this point that our difficulties are more imaginary than real, because a theory of historical interpretation, if it is to claim any justification, must be a well-established empirical hypothesis, based on a close study of the actual facts of historical change. If no such theory has yet succeeded in winning universal acceptance, it can only be a matter of time before one does, and when it does this particular source of disagreement will disappear. But it is by no means certain that this optimistic attitude can be sustained. The paradox of the situation lies, indeed, just in this: that while those who put forward comprehensive theories of this sort profess to derive them from the facts, they hold them with greater confidence than they should if they were merely empirical hypotheses. They are prepared to stand by them even in the face of unfavourable evidence, to accord them the status not so much of hypotheses as of revealed truths. The behaviour of Marxists in regard to the theory of historical materialism is the most obvious illustration of this point, but parallels to it could be found in that of other schools too.

What is the source of the obstinate conviction with which the theories we have mentioned are held or repudiated? In many cases it is no doubt little more than vulgar prejudice. A particular theory strikes us as emotionally as well as intellectually attractive or repulsive, and our attitude to it henceforth is less that of an impartial observer than of a partisan. Our final reason for accepting or rejecting the theory is that we *want* it to be true or false. But it is not clear that this type of explanation covers all cases, and it would certainly not be accepted by sophisticated Marxists, for example. Historical materialism, they would claim, even if not simply grounded in the facts, is none the less capable of rational defence, because we can show it to be bound up with a certain conception of the nature of man and his relation to his environment, a general philosophy whose truth is confirmed in many fields. It is to this philosophy that Marxists make implicit appeal in the course of their historical work, and it is on its validity that the value of their interpretations must finally rest.

If this is correct, it appears that the conflict between different theories of historical interpretation raises no special problems for our purposes. Certainly it is a potent source of disagreement among historians, but the centre of the disagreement, where it cannot be found in simple prejudice, must be looked for in differing philosophical conceptions. Consideration of this third class of subjective factor therefore leads on directly to consideration of the fourth group, to which I shall turn without delay.

(*d*) *Underlying philosophical conflicts.* Since the very title of this section will be viewed with suspicion by hard-headed persons, I must begin by trying to specify more fully what factors fall within the group. What I have in mind are, to make no bones about it, moral and metaphysical beliefs. By the former term I intend to refer to the ultimate judgments of value historians bring to their understanding of the past, by the latter to the theoretical conception of the nature of man and his place in the universe with which these judgments are associated. The two sets of beliefs are, I should say, closely bound up together, though not all who hold them are explicitly aware of the fact.

The suggestion I am making is that historians approach the past each with his own philosophical ideas, and that this has a decisive effect on the way they interpret it. If I am right, differences between historians are in the last resort differences of philosophies, and whether we can resolve them depends on whether we can resolve philosophical conflicts. But I can well imagine that these assertions will involve some strain on the reader's credulity. 'Are you seriously suggesting,' I shall be asked, 'that *all* historians import moral and metaphysical prejudices into their work, thus as it were contemplating the past through spectacles which cannot be removed? And if you are, are you not confusing what is true of history at a crude and unscientific level only with what is true of all history? No doubt ethical, religious or, if you like, metaphysical prejudices can be shown to mar popular historical works of all kinds; but can the same be said of the writings of reputable historians? Is it not apparent that historical thinking can be effective only so far as the historian forgets the ethical, religious and metaphysical outlook of his own age and tries to see his facts in the way those he was writing of did? Must he not read the past in terms, not of his own conception of what human nature is or ought to be, but in terms of the ideas held by those who were alive at the time he is studying? And do we not differentiate good and bad work in history by examining how far particular writers have done just this—by seeing how far they have freed themselves from their own preconceptions and contrived to put themselves in the places of the persons whose actions they are recounting?'

There is obviously much sense in this criticism, yet I doubt even so if it is wholly effective. Certainly there is a difference of the kind indicated between good and bad work in history, a difference we bring out by describing the former as 'authentic' and the latter as 'unimaginative'. Exercising the imagination is an important part of historical thinking, and it does consist in trying, so far as we can, to put ourselves in the places of those whose actions we are studying. But, as we saw before, there are very real difficulties in holding that putting oneself in another man's place is a simple intuitive process: it seems rather to depend on the accumulated experience of the person who carries it out. And when we speak of 'experience' here I think we must recognise that this too is not a simple term. My understanding of the ancient world depends on what I have myself experienced or assimilated from the experience of others; but, as was pointed out in Chapter 3, there seems to be in all such experience a subjective or *a priori* element contributed by myself. When I try to put myself in the place of an ancient Greek or a medieval cleric or a Victorian parent, in order to write the history of the ancient world or the medieval church or the Victorian family, I must certainly put aside, so far as I can, the moral and metaphysical preconceptions of my own time. But I cannot escape, if I am to make any sense of my material, making some general judgments about human nature, and in these I shall find my own views constantly cropping up. I shall find myself involuntarily shocked by this event and pleased by that, unconsciously seeing this action as reasonable and that as the reverse. And however much I tell myself to eschew my own prejudices and concentrate on understanding what actually happened, I shall not succeed in carrying out the injunction to the letter, since understanding itself is not a passive process but involves the judging of evidence by principles whose truth is independently assumed.

The point I am making here will perhaps become plainer for some readers if I try to connect it with the classical discussions of historical testimony to be found in Hume's Essay on Miracles (in his *Enquiry Concerning Human Understanding*) and Bradley's *Presuppositions of Critical History*.[1] Neither Hume nor Bradley is concerned with the whole question of historical objectivity: each of them has in mind only the narrower problem of whether we can believe stories of miraculous events. Even so, their conclusions bear closely on the present discussion. Hume says, in effect, that we cannot give credence to accounts of events in the past the occurrence of which would have abrogated the laws of physical nature; Bradley, urging much the same conclusion, says we can believe about the past only that which bears some analogy to what we know in our own experience. The points in which the present account attempts to go beyond Hume and Bradley are two. First, in suggesting that if we accept Bradley's formula for history we must understand by 'experience' not merely experience of physical nature, but experience of human nature too. And secondly, in maintaining that such experience is not all given, but includes in addition an *a priori* element.

(i) The first of these points should be clear enough from the discussions of Chapter 3, where we tried to show that it was generalisations about human nature which ultimately lay behind historical explanations. It depends on the assertion there made that the proper subject-matter of history is human actions in the past. If this is so it is clear that we must have some knowledge of human nature to make sense of history at all.

(ii) The crucial question is, however, what knowledge we need to have. Here what I am suggesting is that whilst a large part of the content of our conception of human nature is drawn from experience, and alters as our experience is added to, it remains true that there is a hard core in it which is not come by in the same way. This hard core I connect with our moral and metaphysical beliefs. When we look at the past, what understanding we gain of

1. *Collected Essays*, vol. I.

it depends primarily on the extent to which we succeed in identifying ourselves with the subjects of our study, thinking and feeling as they thought. But we could not even begin to understand unless we presupposed some propositions about human nature, unless we applied some notion of what is reasonable or normal in human behaviour. It is here that our own outlook exercises its effect and colours the interpretation we give.

No doubt it is a wise piece of practical advice to historians to tell them to become aware of their own moral and metaphysical preconceptions, and to be on their guard against reading them naïvely into their history. But to draw from that the conclusion that historians have only to make the effort to be able to contemplate the past without any preconceptions, allowing their minds to be coloured solely by what they find there, is surely excessively sanguine. It would certainly be wrong at this stage to infer that objective understanding of the past is impossible, on the ground that we all look at it through our own moral and metaphysical spectacles: the possibility of a synthesis of different points of view, and of the inclusion of one in another, remains to be discussed. Nevertheless, there is without doubt some prima facie case for an ultimate historical scepticism, a case which the spectacle of actual differences among historians greatly strengthens. To ignore this case altogether is to bury one's head in the sand.

§ 4. *Recapitulation*

It may be useful at this point to pause in our argument and see where we stand. In the early part of this chapter we saw that there was some case for saying that every historian looks at the past from his own point of view, an assertion the acceptance of which would appear to commit us to a subjectivist theory of history. But we recognised that the expression, 'a point of view', must itself be subjected to analysis, and the foregoing survey of the main factors which lead historians to disagree was undertaken with that purpose in mind. As a result we are now in a position to see that a 'point of view' is the name of something whose constituent elements are by no means homogeneous. There are some things in our points of view (e.g. our personal likes and dislikes) from which we think we not only can, but must, abstract when we come to write history. But there are also others from which it is altogether harder to abstract—indeed, from which complete abstraction would appear to be impossible—and here the question whether history can provide objective knowledge arises most acutely.

Given that there are elements in a point of view from which abstraction cannot be made, we find ourselves confronted with several alternative theories of history. The first and perhaps the easiest to hold would argue that points of view in the sense we have analysed express subjective attitudes about which argument is futile, and therefore constitute an insurmountable barrier to true knowledge of the past. This is the solution of historical scepticism. The second, which I propose to call the perspective theory, would accept the existence of irreducibly different points of view among historians, but dispute the conclusion that this rules out all objective knowledge of the past. Its contention would be that objectivity in history must be taken in a weakened sense: a history could be said to be objective if it depicted the facts accurately from its own point of view, but not in any other way. And different histories would not contradict, but complement, one another. Finally, there is the theory that objectivity in a strong sense may after all be attainable by historians, since in principle at any rate the possibility of developing a point of view which would win universal acceptance cannot be ruled out.

In the rest of this chapter I must attempt a brief and, I fear, wholly inadequate discussion of these three theories. I shall begin with some remarks about historical scepticism.

§ 5. *Historical scepticism*

Whether any reputable philosopher advocates a thoroughgoing scepticism about historical knowledge I do not know. But Collingwood, however inconsistent it might be with the rest of his theory, came near to doing it,[1] and the position is one which, to anyone who accepted the analysis of different constituents of an historian's point of view given above, would come very naturally. No doubt the denial that objective knowledge of human history is possible involves a large element of paradox; but, as we shall see, an alternative account of the function of history does something to remove this.

1. Compare especially a passage quoted by Professor T. M. Knox on p. xii o his introduction to *The Idea of History*.

I describe historical scepticism as a position which it is very natural for anyone who accepts the above analysis to hold on these grounds. First, because of the view, now so common that it has almost become an article of philosophical orthodoxy, that metaphysical statements are not, as scientific statements are, descriptions of real features of fact, but, at best, expressions of attitudes about which rational argument is impossible. And second, because of the application of a similar analysis to moral statements. Here the case has been much clarified by the distinction drawn by Mr C. L. Stevenson[1] between disagreement in belief and disagreement in attitude. It is pointed out that people who dispute about moral questions may differ either in their description of the facts (i.e. in belief) or in their attitude to them (or in both), and contended that the impression we all have that there is something real to argue about in these matters is to be connected solely with the resolvability of the first kind of dispute. Two people who initially differ about the facts of a moral situation may, given sufficient patience and mental acumen, come to agree about them. But this will not necessarily end the whole dispute. For though changing our assessment of the facts of the situation *may* alter the attitude we take up to it, there is no guarantee that it will. And if it will not, we have to recognise (so it is said) that moral attitudes are not matters of argument at all.

I have no wish to discuss these difficult questions in the present context. My object in including the above paragraph is only to show the non-philosophical reader the background of the view that moral and metaphysical beliefs, so-called, are, strictly speaking, all non-rational: that we hold them not because of any insight into the structure of fact, but simply because we are determined to do so by factors, whether in ourselves or in our environment, over which we have no control. A number of philosophers today would at least be sympathetic to that opinion. But if they are (and this is my point), I think they are in serious danger of committing themselves to an ultimate scepticism about historical knowledge. They must, if my previous contentions are right, recognise that different moral and metaphysical beliefs lie behind different historical interpretations, and they themselves maintain that such beliefs are

1. In his book *Ethics and Language*, ch. I. The distinction was partly anticipated in Hume's moral theory.

not beliefs in the scientific sense, but nothing more than the expressions of non-rational attitudes. It follows that historical thinking will for them have something irreducibly subjective about it, which will inevitably colour any attempted understanding of the past.

Some readers will consider these views so extravagant as not to be worthy of serious consideration. And certainly it must be admitted that to accept them involves accepting the paradox that history is in the last resort not a branch of knowledge at all. But the paradox can be diminished if we offer a different interpretation of history's function. Instead of saying, as we have earlier in this book, that the primary aim of the historian is to discover truth about the past for its own sake, we must now lay stress on history's serving a practical purpose. History, we shall argue, is not so much a branch of science as a practical activity. And we shall ground our assertion on the psychological observation that human beings, in the state of civilisation, feel a need to form some picture of the past for the sake of their own present activities: that they are curious about the past and wish to reconstruct it because they hope to find their own aspirations and interests reflected there. Since their reading of history is determined by their point of view, this requirement is always in some measure fulfilled. But the conclusion we must draw is that history throws light not on 'objective' events, but on the persons who write it; it illuminates not the past, but the present. And that is no doubt why each generation finds it necessary to write its histories afresh.

It may be remarked that the adoption of this view of the function of history is not incompatible with the attaching of great importance to historical studies, as the case of Collingwood, who at least toyed with the idea, shows. On this score, at any rate, the sceptical theory can be defended against criticism. But there is another possible objection to which it is not so easy to see an answer. It is that the theory blurs the distinction all reputable historians draw between history and propaganda, that it confuses (in Professor Oakeshott's language) the 'practical' with the 'historical' past. We saw earlier that historians demand a species of objectivity and impartiality in any historical work which is to deserve its name, and repudiate constructions of the past which simply reflect our emotions or interests as the products of wishful thinking. Such constructions may well have a function (in fact, we all entertain them to some extent), but they are emphatically not history. Yet it might be said that a supporter of the sceptical theory could draw no such conclusion: for him all attempts to reconstruct the past must be propagandist, since they will all aim at helping forward our present activities.

That there is no such thing as history free from subjective prejudice the sceptical theory must certainly allow, and to this extent its supporters must accept the criticism here put forward. But they may none the less seek to evade its difficulties by distinguishing between various kinds, or levels, of propaganda, holding that some kinds are more vicious than others for the historian.

What the suggestion comes to is that we should think of history as being a peculiar sort of game, which we must play according to the rules if we are to play it properly. The trouble about histories which everyone would recognise to be propagandist, on this account, is that those who write them make or break the rules to suit their own ultimate purpose of producing a certain kind of effect, whereas reputable historians think that results achieved in this underhand manner are without value. The situation may be illuminated by reference to the parallel case of artistic activities. An artist who sought only to achieve a certain effect, and cared nothing for the means by which he did it, would be condemned as a charlatan or an exhibitionist by his colleagues. A true artist would not be satisfied to solve his problems except in accordance with the rules of his art. Similarly in history: the 'true', as opposed to the bogus, historian would recognise certain objective rules (respect for the evidence would be an instance) in accordance with which he must argue, and could be marked off by his adherence to those rules. But all this could be maintained without denying that history was primarily a practical activity, or arguing for the objectivity of history in any further sense.

If this distinction is granted, the theory we have been examining certainly becomes much more plausible and attractive. But it may be suggested that to grant the distinction is in fact to have passed to a further view of history altogether—the perspective theory mentioned above. To this I shall now turn.

§ 6. *The perspective theory*

The advocates of the perspective theory agree that every historian contemplates the past from his own standpoint, but they are anxious to add that this does not prevent his attaining some under-standing of what really happened. Their argument for this is the simple one that any finished history is the product of two factors: subjective elements contributed by the historian (his point of view) and the evidence from which he starts, which he must (or rather ought to) accept whether he likes it or not. No doubt the existence of the first factor prevents even the finest historian from reliving the past as it actually was; but it seems absurd to maintain on that ground that his whole reconstruction is radically false. A truer description of the position would be to say that every historian has some insight into what really happened, since to each the past is revealed according to his point of view. The analogy of artistic activity is again useful here. Just as a portrait painter sees his subject from his own peculiar point of view, but would nevertheless be said to have some insight into that subject's 'real' nature, so the historian must look at the past with his own presuppositions, but is not thereby cut off from all understanding of it.

It is important that we should be quite clear just what is being claimed by this theory, and it may be helpful in this connection if we ask in what sense it is possible for a supporter of it to speak of historical truth. The main point to notice here is that the theory forbids us to raise questions about the truth of different points of view in history. If we are asked, 'Which is truer, the Catholic or the Protestant version of the events of the Reformation?' we must reply that we cannot say. There is simply no means of comparing the two accounts, each of which is complete in itself. The Catholic looks at the Reformation from one point of view and offers his interpretation of it; the Protestant looks at it from another and produces a different interpretation. Since points of view are, ultimately, not matters of argument (here the perspectivists join hands with the sceptics), we cannot say that one is 'objectively' better than another, and so must recognise that the Catholic and Protestant versions do not really contradict each other, any more than two portraits of the same man by different artists do. And the same would be said of histories written in different centuries with fundamentally different outlooks. Thus if we hold to this theory there is a sense in which we cannot ask if Mommsen had a truer grasp of the history of Rome than Gibbon: we must say that each wrote with his own presuppositions, and must be judged in terms of these.

Nevertheless, the concepts of truth and objectivity retain in this theory a meaning for the historian. They do so because, inside any given set of presuppositions, historical work can be done more or less well. The history served out by party propagandists to encourage the faithful and convert the wavering is bad history not because it is biased (all history is that), but because it is biased in the wrong way. It establishes its conclusions at the cost of neglecting certain fundamental rules which all reputable historians recognise: scrutinise your evidence, accept conclusions only when there is good evidence for them, maintain intellectual integrity in your arguments, and so on. Historians who neglect these rules produce work which is subjective in a bad sense; those who adhere to them are in a position to attain truth and objectivity so far as these things are attainable in history.

What this comes to is that objectivity in history, according to the perspective theory, is possible only in a weakened or secondary sense. The position can be brought out by once more comparing the notion of scientific objectivity. Scientific results, as we saw, are thought to be objective in the sense that they claim to hold for any observer who sets out from the same body of evidence. Behind the claim lies the idea that the fundamental principles of scientific thinking are the same for all observers, at least at any given stage of scientific development.[1] But historical results cannot be said to have the same validity, if the perspective theory is right. The Marxist interpretation of nineteenth-century political history will be valid, on that view, only for Marxists, the liberal interpretation only for liberals; and so on. But this will not prevent both Marxists and liberals from writing history in a manner which can be called objective: that is to say, from attempting, inside their given presuppositions, to construct an account which really does justice to all the evidence they recognise. There will be relatively objective and relatively subjective Marxist accounts, relatively objective and relatively subjective histories written from the liberal point of view. But there will not be histories which are absolutely objective, in the way scientific theories claim to be.

What are we to say of this theory as a whole? That it has some

[1]. I am assuming that 'Soviet' biology and 'bourgeois' physics are non-existent.

clear merits could certainly not be denied. Thus it is able to recognise certain points of continuity between history and the sciences
(e.g. that they are both primarily cognitive activities) without
losing sight of the important differences between them; in particular,
it does justice to the widespread conviction that there are respects
in which history is to be regarded as an art as well as a science. It
offers an interpretation of historical objectivity which has the
important merit of assigning a special sense to that elusive concept,
instead of fixing its meaning solely by reference to other studies.
And in general it may be said to be altogether more congenial than
the sceptical theory, whose paradoxes undoubtedly lay a considerable strain on human credulity.

Even so, we may well doubt whether the theory gives historians
all they want in the way of an account of historical truth. For,
when all is said, it remains impossible for its supporters to admit
any comparison, other than a purely technical one, between different
versions of the same set of events. Any given history can be
criticised internally, for failing to take proper account of this piece
of evidence or that; but further than this the theory will not let
us go. Yet historians do constantly go further, and think it part of
their proper job that they should do so: they do criticise each other's
presuppositions, and attempt to evaluate different points of view.
They are not content to stop with the recognition of a plurality of
different histories written from different points of view; they
remain obstinately convinced that some points of view are sounder,
nearer the truth, more illuminating, than others. And they believe
they can learn from the interpretations of their fellow historians,
profiting from their mistakes and incorporating in their own work
whatever they find of value there.

It is, of course, perfectly possible that, if historians do make
these assumptions, they are simply deceived; that they are confusing
legitimate with illegitimate criticism, matters which can be argued
about with profit with matters which can not. But the existence of
this possibility will not absolve us from seeing whether an account
of historical objectivity can be devised which will allow for the
claims just made on history's behalf. And indeed we could not
accept the perspective theory with any confidence unless this
alternative had been explored and rejected.

§ 7. *The theory of an objective historical consciousness*

We may begin by noticing an argument which springs from a simple development of the perspective theory and might well be sponsored by many working historians. The argument is that it must be possible for an historian to criticise presuppositions, his own or anyone else's, because their adequacy is clearly shown in the details of historical work. Sets of presuppositions can be pronounced adequate or inadequate, true or false, in so far as they enable us to deal with the evidence on which they are brought to bear. If we work with a bad set of guiding principles we are compelled to distort or suppress evidence in the interests of a preconceived theory, and this violates one of the fundamental rules of historical method. Conversely, a good set of presuppositions will enable us both to cover the available evidence and connect different parts of it together.

Stated thus abstractly, the argument sounds convincing enough; yet we must ask if it does not owe its force to an unconscious assumption which we have already seen reason to doubt. When we say that historical presuppositions can be tested by their ability to do justice to 'the' evidence, of what evidence are we talking? It is all too easy to think that there is a fixed body of evidence for any set of historical events which all historians would recognise, a single datum from which they all start whatever their points of view. But if we do make that assumption, it is one which is not easy to justify. We saw in Chapter 4 that the notion of historical evidence is a difficult one: that whilst historical data are in one sense independent of particular historians, it is also true that historians have to decide what they are to treat as evidence as well as what inferences they are to draw from it. But if this is correct, the perspective theory does not achieve the extension which was promised above. Certainly we must say that no historian can refuse the duty of offering an interpretation of all the evidence he admits, and whether historians do this is at least one of the things we take into account in judging historical work. Yet if any particular writer decides that something is not evidence for him (that, for example, a particular document is a forgery), there is in the last resort nothing anyone else can do about it. And it is just here that the difficulty arises in deciding between conflicting historical interpretations. We cannot, as we are in effect bidden to do, settle the dispute by reference to a body of unassailable fact, because what is fact on one interpretation is not necessarily fact on another. Anyone who reflects on Marxist and anti-Marxist accounts of recent political history should have no difficulty in seeing that.

To advance beyond the foregoing version of the perspective theory by appealing to independent facts is thus not possible. What alternative remains? The only one which occurs to the present writer is that we should hope for the ultimate attainment of a single historical point of view, a set of presuppositions which all historians might be prepared to accept. If this were possible, the problem of objectivity in history would be solved on Kantian lines, by the development of an historical 'consciousness in general', a standard way of thinking about the subject matter of history.

This is a solution which is not new. It was suggested, in effect, by the nineteenth-century positivists when they proposed to make history scientific by resting it on the scientific study of psychology and sociology. It was put forward in a different form by Dilthey in his early and middle periods, when he held that behind history and the human studies generally there lay a fundamental science of human nature, the making explicit of which was an important task for all who had those studies at heart. And it would be a natural development of the account of historical explanation we ourselves offered in Chapter 3 of this book.

Nevertheless, if we are to accept this solution we must do it with our eyes fully open: we must be conscious of its difficulties as well as its attractions. In particular, we must recognise that the carrying out of the positivist programme, as formulated by such writers as Comte, has done little or nothing to bring us nearer agreement on historical questions. If it is too early to speak of our having scientific knowledge of human nature, we might at least claim to have the beginnings of such knowledge. Yet the development of an historical 'consciousness in general', based on a true appreciation of the possibilities of human nature, is still to seek.

Why is this? The answer should be apparent from the argument of this chapter. Roughly speaking, it is that, for objective understanding of the kind contemplated, the historian needs not merely standard knowledge of how people *do* behave in a variety of situations, but further a standard conception of how they *ought* to behave. He needs to get straight not merely his factual knowledge, but also his moral and metaphysical ideas. This important addition was not appreciated by the positivist school.

There are many philosophers today who would say that a programme for providing a standard set of moral and metaphysical ideas is not merely one of extreme difficulty; it is simply impossible of attainment. Our moral and metaphysical ideas (they maintain) spring from non-rational attitudes, and to ask which set of them it is 'rational' to hold is to ask a question which cannot be answered. To this scepticism about moral and metaphysical truth I should not wish to commit myself. I have argued elsewhere[1] that metaphysical disputes may be soluble in principle if not in practice, and I should not be prepared to rule out the possibility of general agreement on moral principles too, about which subject I doubt whether the last word has been said. But even if a solution of these difficult problems can be declared to be not wholly impossible, the achieving of it is clearly not going to be accomplished in the immediate future. Yet until it is accomplished an objective historical consciousness, whose principles would provide a framework for rational thought in history, must remain no more than a pious aspiration. And if it cannot be accomplished we have no alternative but to fall back on the perspective theory discussed above.[2]

1. *Reason and Experience*, ch. X.
2. [The argument of this section is, I fear, seriously confused. Historians certainly need to refer in their work to what is thought normal or appropriate as well as to what regularly occurs; but the thought in question is that of the persons of whom they write, not their own. Hence the problem of a uniform historical consciousness, as presented here, does not arise. For a different way in which the value judgments of historians bear on the question of historical objectivity see Additional Essay (A) below (pp. 169 ff.).]

6

SPECULATIVE PHILOSOPHY OF HISTORY:

KANT AND HERDER

§ 1. *General features*

The term 'philosophy of history' was generally understood a hundred years ago in a sense very different from that given it in the preceding chapters. We have taken it to designate a critical enquiry into the character of historical thinking, an analysis of some of the procedures of the historian and a comparison of them with those followed in other disciplines, the natural sciences in particular. Thus understood, philosophy of history forms part of the branch of philosophy known as theory of knowledge or epistemology. But the conception of it entertained by most writers on the subject in the nineteenth century was entirely different. 'The' philosophy of history, as they called it, had as its object history in the sense of *res gestae*, not *historia rerum gestarum*; and the task of its exponents was to produce an interpretation of the actual course of events showing that a special kind of intelligibility could be found in it.

If we ask why history was thus thought to constitute a problem for philosophers, the answer is because of the apparently chaotic nature of the facts which made it up. To nineteenth-century philosophical eyes history appeared to consist of a chain of events connected more or less loosely or accidentally, in which, at first sight at any rate, no clear plan or pattern could be traced. But to accept that description of history, i.e. to take it at its face value, was for many philosophers of the period a virtual impossibility, for it meant (so they thought) admitting the existence in the of something ultimately unintelligible. To persons brought up to believe with Hegel that the real is the rational and the rational the real, this was a very shocking conclusion to come to, one which ought to be avoided if any way of avoiding it could be found. The way suggested for avoiding it was by the elaboration of a 'philosophy,' or philosophical interpretation, of history which would, it was hoped, bring out the rationality underlying the course of historical events by making clear the plan according to which they had proceeded.

A 'philosophy' of history in this special sense meant, as will be evident, a speculative treatment of detailed historical facts, and as such belonged to metaphysics rather than theory of knowledge. In Hegel himself it was only part of a comprehensive project conceived with incredible boldness—to display the underlying rationality of all sides and aspects of human experience. The philosophy of history took its place in this project alongside the philosophies of nature, art, religion and politics, to all of which the same general treatment was applied.

But though it is with the name of Hegel that this type of speculation is now most readily connected, it would be wrong to suppose that Hegel was its originator. To make such an assumption would, in fact, be doubly erroneous. For firstly, philosophy of history as treated by Hegel in his famous lectures in the 1820's had been familiar to the German public at least for the best part of half a century: Herder, Kant, Schelling and Fichte had all made contributions to it, and their questions and conclusions had a profound effect on Hegel's own views. And secondly, as Hegel well knew, the basic problem with which both he and they were concerned was a very ancient one, which had occurred to philosophers and non-philosophers alike. 'That the history of the world, with all the changing scenes which its annals present,' we read in the concluding paragraph of Hegel's lectures, 'is this process of development and the realisation of Spirit—this is the true Theodicaea, the justification of God in history.' To justify God's ways to man, and in particular to show that the course of history could be interpreted in a manner not inconsistent with accepting divine providence, had been a recognised task for theologians and Christian apologists for many centuries. The writers of the Old Testament had been aware of its importance, it had been treated at length by St Augustine in his *City of God*, and it had provided the theme for Bossuet's *Discourse on Universal History*, published in 1681, as well as for Vico's *New Science* (1725–44). To produce a philosophical interpretation of history along these lines was, it had long been thought, an obvious requirement in any solution of the general metaphysical problem of evil.

Nor is this all. For if these speculations, as the foregoing remarks will suggest, had a theological origin and a recognised place in Christian apologetics, they had their secular counterpart too—in the theories of human perfectibility and progress so dear to the thinkers of the Enlightenment. The writers who, like the French Encyclopaedists, propounded such theories were also in their way engaged on the construction of philosophies of history. They too were attempting to trace a pattern in the course of historical change; they too, to put it very crudely, were convinced that history is going somewhere. And despite their many differences from the theologically-minded, they felt the same need on being confronted with the spectacle of human history, the need to show that the miseries men experienced were not in vain, but were rather inevitable stages on the way to a morally satisfactory goal.

The last point is, I suggest, worth special emphasis, if only because it serves to explain the recurrent interest of philosophy of history of this kind (for example, the interest in Professor Toynbee's writings today). On the face of it the programme mentioned above—the project for penetrating below the surface of history to its hidden meaning—seems scarcely respectable. It savours of a sort of mystical guesswork, and thus has its execution appeared to many hard-headed men. But we miss the point of these enquiries if we leave out of account the main factor which gives rise to them. It is the feeling that there is something morally outrageous in the notion that history has no rhyme or reason in it which impels men to seek for a pattern in the chain of historical events. If there is no pattern, then, as we commonly say, the sufferings and disasters which historians narrate are 'pointless' and 'meaningless'; and there is a strong element in human nature which revolts against accepting any such conclusion. No doubt it is open to critics of the programme to argue that those who devise it are guilty of wishful thinking; but this is a charge which cannot be accepted without an investigation of the results alleged to be achieved.

§ 2. *Kant's philosophy of history*

We must pass from these generalities to particular examples of the speculations in question.

I propose to discuss first the essay contributed by Kant to the periodical *Berlin Monthly*, in November 1784, under the title 'Idea of a Universal History from a Cosmopolitan point of view'; and I must begin by giving reasons for what some may think a curious choice. It could not be claimed for Kant either that he was first in the field in this subject or that his work in it (which amounted in all to no more than two short papers and a lengthy review) was of primary importance in determining the course of subsequent speculation: on both counts he must clearly yield pride of place to Herder. Nor again could it be maintained that Kant had a genuine interest in history for its own sake, or any grasp of the possibilities of historical research: as has often been remarked by critics of his general philosophy, his outlook was singularly unhistorical, and he remained in this as in other respects a typical product of the Enlightenment rather than a forerunner of the Romantic Age which was shortly to follow. But for all that his work on philosophy of history, and in particular the essay we are to study, remains instructive for the modern reader.

It is instructive, I suggest, for two main reasons. First, because it enables us to grasp with singular clarity just what it was that speculative philosophers of history set out to do. Kant's natural modesty and sense of his own limitations make him especially valuable in this connection. He saw that no one could undertake a detailed philosophical treatment of history of the kind he had in mind without a wide knowledge of particular historical facts; and since he made no pretence of having such knowledge himself, he confined himself to sketching the idea of (or, as he put it himself, 'finding a clue to') a philosophy of history, leaving it to others to carry the idea out. In reading Kant on this subject we are not faced, as we are when we read, e.g., Herder or Hegel, with the problem of disentangling a theory from its application, nor with that of making due allowance for inadequate empirical knowledge.

Secondly, Kant's work is instructive because it brings out in an unmistakable way the moral background to this kind of speculation. With him at least philosophy of history was a pendant to moral philosophy; indeed, there is little to suggest that he would have treated of history at all if it were not for the moral questions it seemed to raise. Just what these questions were is indicated with force and clarity more than once in the essay. Thus in the introductory section[1] we read:

One cannot avoid a certain feeling of disgust, when one observes the actions of man displayed on the great stage of the world. Wisdom is manifested by individuals here and there; but the web of human history as a whole appears to be woven from folly and childish vanity, often, too, from puerile wickedness and love of destruction: with the result that at the end one is puzzled to know what idea to form of our species which prides itself so much on its advantages.

And in a later passage[2] he asks:

What use is it to glorify and commend to view the splendour and wisdom of Creation shown in the irrational kingdom of nature, if, on the great stage where the supreme wisdom manifests itself, that part which constitutes the final end of the whole natural process, namely human history, is to offer a standing objection to our adopting such an attitude?

If history is what it appears to be, a belief in divine providence is precluded; yet that belief, or something like it (the argument runs),[3] is essential if we are to lead a moral life. The task of the philosopher as regards history is accordingly to show that, first appearances notwithstanding, history is a rational process in the double sense of one proceeding on an intelligible plan and tending to a goal which moral reason can approve.

How is this result achieved? The 'clue' to the philosophical interpretation of history which Kant has to offer turns out to be very simple: it is, in effect, a variation on the common eighteenth-century theory of progress. History, he suggests, would make sense if it could be seen as a continuous, though not perhaps straightforward, progression towards a better state of affairs. Have

1. Berlin edition of Kant's works, VIII, 17–18.
2. VIII, 30.
3. Compare the argument in § 87 of the *Critique of Judgment*.

we any ground for assuming that such a progression is real?
Certainly not if we confine ourselves to looking at historical
happenings solely from the point of view of the individuals concerned: there we meet with nothing but a chaotic aggregate of
apparently meaningless and unconnected events. But the case may
be different if we transfer our attention from the fortunes of the
individual to that of the whole human species. What from the
point of view of the individual appears 'incoherent and lawless'
may none the less turn out to be orderly and intelligible when
looked at from the point of view of the species; events which
previously seemed to lack all point may now be seen to subserve
a wider purpose. It is after all possible that in the field of history
Nature or Providence (Kant uses the two terms interchangeably)
is pursuing a long-term plan, the ultimate effect of which will be
to benefit the human species as a whole, though at the cost of
sacrificing the good of individual human beings in the process.

We have now to ask whether this is more than an idle possibility.
Kant proceeds to develop an argument to show that we not only
can but must accept the idea. Man has implanted in him (the standpoint adopted is throughout teleological) a number of tendencies
or dispositions or potentialities. Now it would be contrary to
reason (because it would contravene the principle that Nature does
nothing in vain) to suppose that these potentialities should exist
but never be developed, though in the case of some of them (those
particularly connected with reason, e.g. man's inventive faculty)
we can see quite well that the full development cannot take
place in the lifetime of a single individual. We must therefore
imagine that Nature has some device for ensuring that such
potentialities get their development over a long period of time, so
that they are realised so far as the species is concerned, though not
in the case of all its individual members.

The device in question is what Kant calls[1] 'the unsocial sociability'
of man. He explains himself in a passage from which I will quote
at length:

Man has an inclination to associate himself with others, since in such a
condition he feels himself more than man, thanks to his being able to
develop his natural capacities. On the other hand he also has a strong
propensity to cut himself off (isolate himself) from his fellows, since he

1. op. cit., VIII, 20.

finds in himself simultaneously the anti-social property of wanting to order everything according to his own ideas; as a result of which he everywhere expects to meet with antagonism, knowing from his own experience that he himself is inclined to be antagonistic to others. Now it is this antagonism which awakens all the powers of man, forces him to overcome his tendency to indolence and drives him, by means of the desire for honour, power or wealth, to procure for himself a position among his fellows, whom he can neither get on with nor get on without. Thus it is that men take the first real steps from the state of barbarism to that of civilisation, which properly consists in the social worth of man; thus it is that all talents are gradually developed, that taste is formed, and a beginning made towards the foundation of a way of thinking capable of transforming in time the rude natural tendency to moral distinctions into determinate practical principles: that is to say, capable of converting in the end a social union originating in pathological needs into a moral whole. But for these anti-social properties, unlovely in themselves, whence springs the antagonism every man necessarily meets with in regard to his own egoistic pretensions, men might have lived the life of Arcadian shepherds, in perfect harmony, satisfaction and mutual love, their talents all remaining for ever undeveloped in the bud.[1]

It is, in fact, precisely the bad side of human nature—the very thing which causes us to despair when we first survey the course of history—which Nature turns to account for the purpose of leading man from the state of barbarism into that of civilisation.

The transition is, or rather (since it is not supposed to be complete) will be, effected in two main stages. The first consists of a passage from the state of nature to that of civil society. But not every form of civil society is adequate for the purpose Kant has in mind: a despotic or totalitarian community, for example, would not be suitable. What is needed is a society which, as he himself puts it, 'combines with the greatest possible freedom, and in consequence antagonism of its members, the most rigid determination and guarantee of the limits of this freedom, in such a way that the freedom of each individual may coexist with that of others.'[2] What is needed, in fact, is a liberal society, with full play for private enterprise. But it is not enough (and here we pass to the second stage of the transition) for this ideal to be realised in a single community. The situation, familiar to the readers of Hobbes, of

1. VIII, 20–22.
2. VIII, 22.

the war of individuals against each other is repeated, as Hobbes also saw, in the international sphere; and the attainment of a perfect civil society requires a regulation of international as well as national affairs. Hence we must suppose that the final purpose of Nature in the sphere of history is the establishment of a confederation of nations with authority over all its members, and that it is to this goal that men will finally be driven by the miseries its absence brings about. But it should be noted that these miseries, the most prominent of which is war, are not themselves wholly pointless: on the contrary, war stimulates men to exertions and discoveries they would otherwise not have made, and so contributes to the realisation of Nature's design. And even when an international authority is set up Kant clearly does not think of nations as losing their identity and ceasing to emulate one another; otherwise, as he points out, 'the powers of the human race will go to sleep.'[1]

'The history of the human species as a whole may be regarded as the realisation of a secret plan of Nature for bringing into existence a political constitution perfect both from the internal point of view and, so far as regards this purpose, from the external point of view also: such a constitution being the sole condition under which Nature can fully develop all the capacities she has implanted in humanity.'[2] This is the conclusion drawn by Kant from the foregoing arguments, and offered by him as a clue to the construction of a philosophy of history. That the argument which leads up to it is in large part *a priori* he has no wish to deny. Will an empirical survey of the actual course of events confirm the reliability of these *a priori* speculations? Wisely pointing out that the period for which we have historical records is too short for us to hope to trace in it anything like the general form which history as a whole must take, Kant nevertheless holds that the evidence, as far as it goes, does confirm his suggestions. But he leaves it to others better versed in the subject than himself to write a universal history from the philosophical point of view, merely remarking that his putting the project forward is in no way intended to detract from the prosecution of historical studies by empirical means. It is not a short cut to the discovery of historical facts he is offering; merely a way of looking at the facts once they are discovered.

1. VIII, 26.
2. VIII, 27.

§ 3. Criticism of Kant's theory

So much by way of summary of Kant's theory; we must now turn from exposition to evaluation.

I shall begin with a point which will readily occur to readers of the preceding pages: the external character of Kant's approach to history. I refer to the fact that there is on his theory a complete gulf between the activity of the historian discovering facts about the past and that of the philosopher devising a point of view from which sense can be made of them. The philosopher, it appears, can produce a rationale of history without taking any account of the detailed course of historical change. His standpoint is reached by the combination of a number of *a priori* principles (such as that Nature does nothing in vain) with certain broad generalisations about human behaviour, generalisations which may be confirmed by a scrutiny of historical records but are not necessarily arrived at by processes of historical research. And the comment we must make on this is that though Kant puts his standpoint forward as one from which some future historian may attempt a satisfactory universal history, it is by no means clear that the project will have any appeal to working historians. For if we are assured in advance of experience (and in some sense we are assured, though the point, as we shall see, is a difficult one) that history does and must conform to a certain pattern, what incentive is there to undertake the laborious task of tracing that pattern empirically?

Two possible ways of meeting this difficulty must now be considered.

First, it might be urged that the *a priori* knowledge Kant is ascribing to the philosopher of history is on his own account very limited in scope, and so far from constituting a bar to positive historical enquiry ought rather to act as a stimulus to it. The argument for its so doing would depend for its plausibility on appeal to a parallel case—that of the philosophy of nature. In the *Critique of Pure Reason* and elsewhere Kant tried to show that there were certain propositions of a very general kind which philosophers could assert about nature independently of experience, and argued that the knowledge of these propositions was a positive encouragement to empirical enquiry (for instance, the conviction that nature is orderly stimulated Kepler to further investigations in the face of discouraging results). Similarly, it might be said, knowledge of the proposition that there is a certain pattern in the historical process should encourage historians to pursue their studies, much as the conviction that there is a way out of a maze encourages the lost to go on looking for it.

But this line of defence fails when we observe that the parallel adduced is not strictly accurate. The 'universal laws of nature,' of which Kant claims in the *Critique of Pure Reason* that we have *a priori* knowledge and of which the general law of causality is the best-known instance, are one and all formal principles: they are of use in enabling us to anticipate, not the details, but only the general form of experience. By knowing the principle that every event has a cause, for instance, we know nothing about the causal connections between particular events; we know only that it is reasonable to look for causes whenever we meet with natural events. To put the point another way, from the proposition that all events have causes nothing follows about the particular causal relations we shall meet with in nature. But the principle taken for granted by the Kantian philosopher of history is in this respect quite different; for when we are assured of that principle, as Kant thinks we are, we are assured not merely that there is a pattern in history but further that it is a pattern *of a certain kind*. In other words, the principle assumed in Kant's philosophy of history is a material principle, and it is just because of this that its relation to the assertions of working historians is of importance.

We are therefore driven back on the alternative line of defence, to which I shall make a somewhat devious approach.

It is a common practice among philosophers today to follow Leibniz in dividing true propositions into truths of fact and truths of reason. Truths of fact are validated or confuted by reference to particular experiences; truths of reason, about the nature and number of which there is much controversy, are agreed to be valid irrespective of what in particular occurs. Now the question might be asked into which class we should put the principle of the Kantian philosopher of history (if we can refer in this way to the sentence quoted on p. 125 above). The answer is not easy to find. For on the one hand we must say that the principle looks like a factual truth, since, as we have just seen, it concerns not the form but, in a wide sense, the matter of experience. On the other hand it seems reasonably clear that Kant did not envisage the possibility that it was open to confutation by experience, but regarded it as resting on *a priori* grounds; and in this respect it looks like a truth of reason.

What this suggests is that the status of Kant's principle, and our supposed knowledge of it, require more careful investigation than we have hitherto given to them. And when we compare what he has to say about history with some of his other doctrines (notably those in the appendix to the Dialectic in the *Critique of Pure Reason* and those in the *Critique of Judgment*) we see that he is in fact assigning a special standing to the principle he has sought to establish. He regards it, in fact, neither as an empirical proposition nor as a necessary truth in the sense in which the general law of causality is for him a necessary truth, but rather as what he calls in the first *Critique* a regulative or heuristic principle, useful in the prosecution of empirical research but not itself susceptible of any kind of proof. And for that reason it is not, in the strict sense, 'known' to anyone. The only propositions which, in Kant's view, we can be said to know are, on the one hand, propositions concerning matters of fact, on the other propositions such as the 'universal laws of nature' mentioned above; and the principle with which we are concerned falls into neither class. It is a principle of whose truth we can have subjective but not objective certainty; we can be assured of it, thanks to its being closely involved in moral practice,[1] but more than that we cannot claim.

Recognition of these subtleties puts Kant's case in a different light; yet even so the position is not wholly clear. We are now being invited to believe that the principle which guides the philosophical historian is a heuristic principle, which would assign it the same status as, for example, the principle of teleology, to which, Kant thought, working biologists must make appeal. When we adopt that principle we direct our scientific studies on the assumption that nature is working purposively, at any rate in regard to some of her products; and this is (or may be) an important step on the road to scientific discovery. If this parallel can be justified—if we can show that there is a precise analogy between what the historian gets and what the biologist gets from philosophy—then Kant's contention is at any rate a respectable one. Unfortunately

1. See the section of the *Critique of Pure Reason* entitled 'On Opinion, Knowledge and Belief' (B848/A820).

here again the parallel suggested does not seem to be exact. The trouble is that Kant is claiming that philosophers can provide working historians not merely with a general principle (as they can provide working biologists with the general principle of teleology), but with a special principle of a particular kind. If I am warranted in assuming the teleological principle in nature I am warranted in expecting that I shall meet in nature with examples of purposive behaviour; and I plan my researches accordingly. What I have done is to accept teleology as a methodological postulate or working assumption. But an assumption of that kind does not lead me to anticipate finding any particular sort of purposive pattern in nature. By contrast, if I accept the Kantian principle of historical interpretation, I am able to say, without reference to experience, not only that history has a plot, but also, in general terms, what that plot is. As we saw before, it is not only the form of experience that Kant's principle enables me to anticipate, but, to an important extent, its matter too; and this it is which makes everyday historians suspicious of the Kantian account.

It is useless in this connection to point out that, if we follow Kant strictly, we cannot be said to 'know' in advance of experience the general plot to which history may be expected to conform. We do indeed lack scientific knowledge of it, just as we do of other principles of the heuristic kind; but this has no bearing on the situation. For the fact remains that on Kant's view we are well assured of the principle in question. We may not be able to prove it, but that does not mean that it is open to doubt.

I conclude that though the Kantian doctrine is a great deal more complex and more subtle than might appear at first sight, it is nevertheless one which historians would find difficult to characterise as other than arbitrary. The problem for a theory of this type is to give an account of the relation of the *a priori* to the empirical elements in philosophical history, to avoid the easily proffered reproach that the philosophical historian is merely making the facts up, or selecting them, to suit his own wishes. It does not seem to me that Kant has an adequate answer to this problem, though he was acutely aware of the general problem of which it is a specification. Nor is it comforting to observe that parallel difficulties are to be found in regard to Hegel's philosophy of history, as we shall presently see.

In the above remarks I have concentrated exclusively on the epistemological side of Kant's theory of history. I should add at this point that there are critics such as Mr Carritt,[1] who have attacked Kant's views on moral grounds as well, urging that history cannot have a moral point if it demands (as Kant seems to be saying) so many innocent victims in the accomplishment of its goal. But this is a charge which I shall not discuss, since in my view Kant's theory falls to the ground independently of whether it can be met successfully or not.

§ 4. *Herder's philosophy of history*

To pass from the writings of Kant to those of Herder, the next author to be considered, is to pass from one age to another; though in fact the first part of Herder's *magnum opus, Ideas for a Philosophical History of Mankind,* appeared a few months earlier than the essay we have just been examining. Herder had been in his youth a pupil of Kant's, but the mature ideas and outlook of the two men could scarcely have been more opposed. Kant, born in 1724, was a product of the Enlightenment: cool and critical in temper, cautious in speculation and suspicious of all forms of mysticism, he was touched only slightly[2] by the upsurge of Romanticism which had so profound an effect on German intellectual life in the closing years of the eighteenth century. But Herder was born twenty years later; he was a man of sensibility rather than cold intellect; speculation and passion were in his blood. It was scarcely surprising in these circumstances that he came to despise the precise Kantian antitheses of empirical and *a priori*, content and form, with all the conclusions Kant had drawn from them about the competence of the human mind to acquire knowledge. By nature it was in intuition rather than discursive intellect that he felt inclined to put his trust. As might be expected, his results, whilst at times brilliant and suggestive, were at others extraordinarily odd.

Herder's masterpiece (for so, despite everything, it must be

---

1. E. F. Carritt; *Morals and Politics* (1947).
1. That he did feel its influence in some degree could not be denied: the *Critique of Judgment* (in particular, the discussion of teleology, which greatly interested Goethe) bears witness to that. But when he does speculate he is always careful to point out the hazardous character of his own procedure, and it is in this that he differs from his immediate successors.

called) is a difficult work to summarise. It is, to begin with, un-
finished (of the twenty-five 'books' planned, the last five were not
written); but that is perhaps the least of its difficulties. The main
trouble is the very broad way in which Herder conceives his
subject. Unlike Kant, he proposes to write philosophical history,
not merely to discuss its possibility; and in due course he begins
to carry the proposal into effect. But before reaching that stage the
reader has to work through no less than ten books of preliminary
matter, covering a wide variety of topics, and in effect constituting
a philosophical treatise in themselves.

Herder's defence of his procedure would be that if we are to
understand human history we must first understand man's place
in the cosmos, and take the subject pretty seriously. Just how
seriously he takes it himself is shown by the fact that he begins
with a disquisition on the physical character of the earth and its
relation to other planets. Thence he proceeds to a survey of plant
and animal life, with a view to elucidating the special characteristics
of the human species. The most arresting of these characteristics,
in Herder's opinion, is man's upright station, the fact that, unlike
any other animal, he walks on two legs: to this feature he attributes
an astonishing variety of human phenomena: not merely the
development of reasoning powers by human beings (their upright
posture affecting their brains) and their use of language, but
(amongst other things) their having moral and religious faculties.
But all this is only a preliminary to a still broader piece of speculation. Herder is impressed by the fact that there is a continuous
series of gradations from the simplest form of inorganic matter
to man, the highest, because the most complex, form of animal
life; and he propounds the hypothesis that the whole universe is
animated by a single organising force, or unified set of organising
forces, working for the free emergence of spirit. Man is the highest
product of this life force (for so it may be called) on the earth, and
all else there exists to subserve his development; but it would be
wrong to think of him as the only spiritual creature in the universe.
On the contrary, everything goes to suggest that he stands half-way
between two worlds, forming the connecting link between them:
a world of animal beings of which he is the highest member, and
one of spiritual beings of which he is the lowest.

This takes us to the end of Book V. The remainder of the

introduction (Books VI–X) is less exciting, but nearer the main topic of the work, covering as it does such subjects as the influence of geography and climate on history, and the differentiation of races. History, for Herder, is a resultant of the interplay of two sets of forces: the external forces which constitute human environment, and an internal force which can only be described as the spirit of man or, more accurately, as the spirit of the various peoples into which the homogeneous human species is broken up. To understand the history of a nation we must certainly take account of its geographical and climatic background; but we cannot hope, as some writers have done, to explain its whole development in these terms. On the contrary, we must recognise that every nation is animated by a certain spirit, which finds expression in whatever its members do.

The importance of this idea should not be judged by the crudity of its present expression. In putting it forward Herder was not only pointing out the unsatisfactoriness of any purely materialistic theory of history; he was also taking an important step towards breaking away from the unhistorical outlook characteristic of his age. It was common in the eighteenth century to think of human nature as a constant, which did not vary fundamentally but merely behaved differently in different circumstances. The important distinction between men, it was thought, was that between civilised and barbarian; but civilised men were the same at all times and in all places. Now this assumption had important practical effects— it meant, for instance, that Orientals were treated on their merits, without racial prejudice; but its bearing on historical studies was less fortunate. It fostered an attitude to the past which was altogether too uncritical and simple-minded. Herder's observation,[1] obvious as it seems today, that the histories of Greece and China would not have taken the courses they did if the Greeks had lived in China and the Chinese in Greece, drew attention to this uncritical spirit, and in so doing made possible the modern concept of civilisation as being, not uniform and unchanging, but differently specified among different peoples.[2]

The details of Herder's treatment of the facts of world history,

1. *Ideas*, Book XIII, ch. VII.
2. Herder, in fact, may be said to have invented the idea of *a* civilisation as opposed to that of civilisation itself. Alternatively, we might ascribe to him the notion of national character.

which occupies the remainder of the *Ideas*, need not detain us, though it is worth remarking that his way of organising his material seems to have been the model followed by Hegel. Of more interest are the general reflections with which he intersperses his narrative at regular intervals, for it is in these that what he himself takes to be the philosophical lessons of history are brought out. In seeking for a philosophy of history he seems, to judge from these passages, to have been doing two things. First, to have tried to show that historical events are not lawless, but proceed according to laws just as natural events do. To this end he reiterates constantly the assertion that the key to any historical situation is to be found in the circumstances (including the internal circumstances mentioned above) in which it took place: we have only to enumerate those circumstances, discover the forces at work, to see that things must have happened in the way they did. The flowering of a civilisation is for Herder as natural as the flowering of a rose, and an appeal to the notion of the miraculous is no more needed in the first case than the second. And secondly, to have tried to discover a general purpose in history, something to lend point to the whole historical process. Such a purpose, he argues,[1] cannot be thought of satisfactorily (here once more we meet with the moral twist of speculative philosophy of history) as something external to man: man's destiny must lie in his own potentialities. Somewhat vaguely, Herder announces that the purpose of history is the attainment of humanity, i.e. (presumably) the attainment of a state of affairs where men are most truly themselves. And he speaks at times as if this was an end which men could deliberately help to bring about; though how that could be if things must happen as they do is not apparent.

Herder's conclusion is thus not substantially different from Kant's, though he would not himself have liked the comparison. His reaction to Kant's theory would be to condemn it as *a priori*, a piece of metaphysics in a sense of the term thought disreputable then as now. His own views, by contrast, claimed to be grounded in a careful scrutiny of the facts. But we may well ask whether Herder is not perhaps too sanguine in this matter. Like other writers of a speculative turn of mind, he starts from the facts, but uses them as a springboard rather than a final resting-place, devel-

1. Book XV. ch. I.

oping analogies and bold hypotheses in a way which strikes more sober persons as unwarranted. The criticism that greater caution was needed struck him, when it was made by Kant,[1] as the reaction of a narrow and unimaginative mind, one which lacked the insight necessary for the philosophical understanding of history. It is on the genuineness or otherwise of the insight here claimed that Herder must finally be judged.

---

1. In his reviews (Berlin edition, VIII, 43–66) of the first two parts of the *Ideas*, the sceptical tone of which mortally offended the author.

7

SPECULATIVE PHILOSOPHY OF HISTORY:

HEGEL

§ 1. *Transition to Hegel*

The purpose of the present discussions is to illustrate the character of speculative philosophy of history, not to write a complete history of the subject. I shall accordingly omit at this point all reference to such writers as Schelling and Fichte, and proceed at once to an examination of the relevant views of Hegel, despite the fact that there is a fifty-year gap between the publication of Herder's *Ideas* and that of Hegel's *Lectures on the Philosophy of History*. The transition need not, however, appear unduly abrupt, since Hegel's theories can easily be represented as continuous with those we have just considered. Hegel, indeed, might well have claimed to have embodied the virtues of both his predecessors, combining the passion and strength of imagination admired by Herder with the precision of mind demanded by Kant.[1]

To expound and comment on Hegel's philosophy of history in a few pages is an undertaking which requires some boldness, since it involves giving a sketch, however briefly, of the Hegelian philosophy as a whole. As was pointed out at the beginning of Chapter 6, history is only one of a series of fields which Hegel proposes to 'comprehend' rationally; and it is the general principle

1. According to Hegel, Kant's philosophy embodied the outlook of the scientific understanding, whilst Herder belonged to the reaction against that outlook which expressed itself in the Romantic philosophies of feeling. Hegel's own philosophy was intended to synthesise these two in a new standpoint, that of speculative reason. See further below.

behind this activity which we must attempt to make clear, as well as its particular application. But before following this procedure we must put in an important proviso. In Hegel's completed system the march of history is explained as a dialectical progress; and to understand dialectic we are referred to the most abstract of all philosophical disciplines, namely logic. This may suggest that we can immediately object to Hegel, as we did to Kant, that the standpoint he adopts towards history is an external one; and the criticism must, indeed, in some measure be sustained. But it is important to notice that the logical order of Hegel's writings does not correspond with the historical order of his own philosophical development. Everything goes to show that the problems which preoccupied him in the years when his views were maturing were not questions of abstract logic and metaphysics, but much more concrete issues, in particular the question of the philosophical interpretation of the nature and history of religion.[1] It is thus misleading to suggest that Hegel first worked out the dialectic *a priori* and then proceeded to apply it, Procrustes-like, to the sphere of empirical fact. Whatever the truth of the matter in other fields, it is clear enough that in the case of history a genuine interest in the facts preceded the discovery of their dialectical connections.

§ 2. *Dialectic and the philosophy of spirit*

Be this as it may, Hegel's philosophy of history can be understood only if it is located within a wider context, and we must begin by giving some account of that context. The philosophical sciences, as Hegel called them, comprised two main divisions: logic, or the science of the Idea, and the philosophies of Nature and Spirit, the sciences of the concrete embodiment of the Idea. Logic dealt with the formal articulation of the concepts of pure reason, those concepts which (Hegel thought) were predicable not of particular things or classes of things, but of reality viewed as a whole. There were certain predicates (in a wide sense of the term) such as 'existence' and 'measurability', which applied, or were thought to apply, to whatever is; and logic, conceived on this view quite differently from the formal logic of tradition, was said to be the

1. Compare the works (not published by Hegel himself) from the period 1795–1800, translated by T. M. Knox and R. Kroner in *Hegel's Early Theological Writings*.

study of these crucial predicates. Its aim was to establish both what concepts fell into this particular class and how they were connected together.

Both problems, in Hegel's view, could be solved, thanks to the dialectical nature of thought. It is extremely important that the reader should have some idea of what is meant by 'dialectic' in this context. One way of approaching this very difficult subject is by considering the way in which the concepts of pure reason are held to form, not merely a series, but a self-generating series. Suppose we employ one of the concepts in question in an effort to make a satisfactory statement about reality as a whole; suppose, for example, we judge that the real is the measurable. Then, it is said, reflection on the concept employed will, if sufficient attention is given to the question, reveal certain inadequacies or contradictions in it; and this will lead us not merely to abandon the judgment that the real is the measurable, but to commit ourselves to the opposite point of view, that the concept of measurement cannot be properly applied to reality at all. We might reach this position if we argued, for instance, that to measure anything involves breaking it up into separate parts, whilst one feature which we know reality to possess from our immediate experience is continuity.

But the new judgment, when we scrutinise it carefully, turns out to be no more satisfactory than the first: it too involves us in difficulties and contradictions. To say that reality is beyond measure is as misleading as to say that it is essentially capable of measurement; the truth is that we want to make both assertions at once. We are therefore led to make a fresh characterisation of reality which will do justice to the good points, and avoid the errors, of both. Should we attain to this new point of view (and Hegel holds that its attainment is always in principle possible) thought has made a definite advance; but it does not follow that it has attained permanent satisfaction. On the contrary: the whole process will repeat itself, and a fresh series of ideas be produced, when the resulting concept is critically examined.

To say that the concepts of pure reason, the categories or *Denkbestimmungen*, as Hegel called them, are dialectically related is to call attention to this peculiar property they have of giving rise one to another. The contention is that their content is such that they fall naturally into triads of thesis, antithesis and synthesis, and that the synthesis-concept of each triad becomes a thesis-concept for a new triad. And it is perhaps worth noticing in this connection that the relationship is said to hold in the first instance not between facts or events, but between concepts or ideas. In current politics we hear much of the alleged 'contradictions' of capitalism, and it is to the Hegelian logic that this way of speaking must be traced back; but it was not to this sort of sphere that the dialectic was originally applied at all.

The business of logic, as conceived by Hegel, is to follow the dialectic to its conclusion; it can be carried out because it is possible to assign an upper and a lower limit to the series of ideas through which thought naturally passes. There can be no idea more simple than that of pure being; and when the thinker arrives at the notion of the Absolute Idea, as the culminating category is called, there is no further step in the field of logic for him to take.

But here the words 'in the field of logic' must be emphasised. When the logician finally attains the notion of the Absolute Idea he has, as a logician, done everything that is required of him: he has followed out the whole dialectical progress of the categories, and no further contradictions confront him. But Hegel holds that his satisfaction will even so not be complete. For he will be troubled by the abstract character of *all* the ideas studied by logic; he will want to show that their content exists, not merely in some sort of Platonic heaven, but also, and properly, in the world of fact. He will be confronted in effect with the problems of the philosophies of Nature and Spirit, that of the concrete or 'phenomenal' embodiment of the Idea.

It is highly important for the understanding of Hegel's attitude to history to grasp, in a general way at least, what lies behind this strange-sounding notion. Perhaps we can make it clear, or clearer, by the following considerations.

Reality for Hegel is spirit: the universe is, in a sense, the product of mind and therefore intelligible to mind. Hegel's philosophy is thus rightly characterised by the epithet 'rationalist.' But we must ask *what* mind cognizes when it tries to think the world. So far as logic is concerned, all it would seem to grasp is a series of purely general characters, merely possible predicates whose attribution to concrete situations is wholly contingent. Thus what logic appears to present us with is, in the picturesque words of Bradley, 'a ghostly

ballet of bloodless categories'. Such a result struck others besides
Bradley as a cheat and a sham, among them Hegel himself. In his
own day Hegel saw the way the abstract conception of reason
favoured by Kant and (in general) the pre-Kantian rationalists
had been countered by the many philosophies of feeling; and hostile
as he was to those philosophies, he was anxious to incorporate in
his own system the truth he held them to embody. It was to this
end that he tried to devise a new form of rationalism, one for which
specifically rational concepts were something more than empty
abstractions, one which looked on ideas as in some way containing
the seed of their development in the concrete. If such a standpoint
could be justified, the categories might be shown to have blood
in them after all, and the reproaches of the philosophers of feeling
be answered.

It was this need to avoid an abstract rationalism which led Hegel
to take the step we are endeavouring to explain. So far we have
spoken as if dialectic were confined to the sphere of logic; and this
was indeed its original home. But now we learn that, in addition
to all the internal triads of logic, logic or the Idea is itself part of a
super-triad, of which Nature forms the antithesis and Spirit (mental
life) the synthesis. The Idea, to be fully itself, demands concrete
embodiment, which it finds by 'externalising' itself as Nature and
'returning to' itself as Concrete Spirit.

It follows from this that the key to the philosophical understanding of empirical facts, whether of the natural or the mental
world, is to be found for Hegel in the categories of his logic, and
that the dialectical transitions of the latter find their counterpart
in the former. But the relationship should not be misunderstood.
Though Hegel would probably accept the statement just made,
he would protest with the utmost vigour against any attempt to
represent him as holding that the world of fact is but a pale reflection
of the world of intellectual ideas. That sort of view had been held
by previous philosophers with whom he had some affinity, for
example by Plato; but it was emphatically not Hegel's view. For
him Nature and Spirit were not mere imitations of the logical Idea,
they were developments of it; and that meant that to understand
them something more was required than knowledge of the Idea.
In other words, for Hegel as for the rest of us the suggestion that
philosophers might deduce empirical truths *a priori* was absurd.

Logic could offer the philosopher a guiding-thread through the labyrinth of experience, but it could not serve as a substitute for experience itself.

§ 3. *Hegel's philosophy of history*

The reader should now be in a position to consider some of the details of Hegel's treatment of history.

Philosophy of history, for Hegel, is part of the philosophy of Spirit, and the problem which confronts its exponent is that of tracing the working of reason in a particular empirical sphere. That reason is at work in history—that in this as in other fields the real is the rational—is a proposition which the philosophical historian does not undertake to prove or even examine: he takes it as demonstrated by logic or, as we should prefer to say, metaphysics. His task is to apply the principle, showing that an account of the facts can be given consistently with it.

This gives us the differentia of philosophical as opposed to empirical or everyday history. Ordinary historians, whether they are 'original' writers like Thucydides and Julius Caesar, confining themselves for the most part to the narrative of contemporary events, or 'reflective' historians painting on a broader canvas such as Livy, feel their first duty to be the accurate delineation of the facts. They may brighten up their narrative by presenting it from a distinct point of view, or they may season it with reflections of topical interest; but particular facts remain their paramount concern. The philosophical historian, by contrast, is struck by the fragmentary and inconsequential character of the results thus achieved, and looks for something better. This something better is the divination of the meaning and point of the whole historical process, the exhibition of reason's working in the sphere of history. To accomplish this task the philosopher must take the results of empirical history as data, but it will not suffice for him merely to reproduce them. He must try to illuminate history by bringing his knowledge of the Idea, the formal articulation of reason, to bear upon it, striving, in a phrase Hegel uses elsewhere,[1] to elevate empirical contents to the rank of necessary truth.

This sounds an imposing and exciting programme, but before

1. *Encyclopaedia*, § 12 (*The Logic of Hegel*, translated by W. Wallace, p. 19).

we attempt to discuss it we must sketch Hegel's theories in a little more detail.

The clue to history, in Hegel's view, is to be found in the idea of freedom. 'World History', in the words of the lectures, 'exhibits the development of the consciousness of freedom on the part of Spirit, and of the consequent realisation of that freedom.'[1] This principle is capable both of abstract logical proof and of empirical confirmation. Historical phenomena, as we know, are manifestations of Spirit as opposed to Nature (though Hegel does not overlook the importance of the natural background to men's actions), and

It is a result of speculative philosophy that freedom is the sole truth of Spirit. Matter possesses gravity in virtue of its tendency towards a central point. It is essentially composite, consisting of parts which exclude each other. It seeks its unity, and therefore exhibits itself as self-destructive, as verging towards its opposite. If it could attain this it would be matter no longer, it would have perished. It strives after the realisation of its idea; for in unity it exists ideally. Spirit on the contrary may be defined as that which has its centre in itself. It has not a unity outside itself, but has already found it; it exists in and with itself. Matter has its essence out of itself. Spirit is self-contained existence. Now this is freedom exactly.[2]

A glance at the actual course of historical events confirms these abstract considerations. In the Oriental World (the civilisations of China, Babylonia and Egypt) despotism and slavery were the rule: freedom was confined to a single man, the monarch. But the Greco-Roman world, although retaining the institution of slavery, extended the area of freedom, claiming it as the right of citizens if not of all individuals. The process has been completed by the Germanic nations of modern Europe, who have accepted the Christian principle of the infinite worth of individual men as such, and so have explicitly adopted the idea of liberty; though, as Hegel notes, this does not mean that they have carried it to full effect in their institutions.

It remains to determine in what sense 'freedom' is to be understood in this account; but the main lines of Hegel's attitude are

1. *Lectures on the Philosophy of History*, translated by J. Sibree (Bohn's Libraries), p. 66.
2. op. cit., p. 18.

already clear. Like Kant and the philosophers of the Enlightenment, he is proposing to 'make sense' of history by means of the notion of progress; he differs from them only in importing the dialectic, thus professing to give the theory an *a priori* ground.

We must now enquire into the stages of the progression of which history, in Hegel's view, consists. Here he shows signs of having learnt from both his main predecessors. From Kant he takes over the notion that philosophical history must concern itself with some larger unit than individual men, and he identifies this unit, following Herder, with different nations or peoples. Every nation has its own characteristic principle or genius, which reflects itself in all the phenomena associated with it, in 'its religion, its political institutions, its moral code, its system of law, its *mores*, even its science and art, and the level of mechanical aptitude it attains.'[1] And every nation has a peculiar contribution which it is destined, in its turn, to make to the process of world history. When a nation's hour strikes, as it does but once, all other nations must give way to it, for at that particular epoch it, and not they, is the chosen vehicle of the world spirit.'[2]

A philosophical approach to history thus puts us in possession (*a*) of the main *motif* of the drama of which history consists, and (*b*) of the fact that the drama is divided into distinct acts. Can it take us any further? Here Hegel is for a moment cautious. 'That such and such a specific quality constitutes the peculiar genius of a people,' he says,[3] 'is the element of our enquiry which must be derived from experience and historically proved.' As we saw before, philosophy does not profess to be able to anticipate the details of experience. But it seems all the same to have something to tell us about them, for the passage immediately continues: 'to accomplish this presupposes, not only a disciplined faculty of abstraction, but an intimate acquaintance with the Idea.' And in the *Philosophy of Right*,[4] where the contents of the lectures are anticipated in summary form, we are offered an argument which purports not only to show that the main stages of the historical process must be four in number (corresponding to the four 'world-historical' realms, Oriental, Greek, Roman and Germanic, which empirical enquiry

1. op. cit., pp. 66–7.
2. cf. *Philosophy of Right*, § 347.
3. *Lectures*, p. 67.
4. *Philosophy of Right*, §§ 352–3.

establishes), but further to deduce *a priori* the main characteristics of each.

There is one further feature of Hegel's philosophy of history which no account of it, however brief, should omit: his doctrine of the moving forces in historical change. Here too he appears to be indebted, in an unexpected way, to Kant. Just as Kant had argued (cf. p. 123 above) that Providence takes advantage of the bad side of human nature to accomplish its purposes in history, so Hegel contends that reason's great design can be carried out only with the co-operation of human passions. Certain individuals, great men like Caesar or Alexander, are chosen instruments of destiny. They pursue their purposes, seeking each his individual satisfaction, but in doing this produce results of a far-reaching importance they could not themselves have foreseen. Such men are indispensable if the plot of history is to be worked out, for ideas are impotent until will-power stands behind them. Hegel adds that they must not in consequence be judged by ordinary moral standards:

Such men may treat other great, even sacred, interests inconsiderately; conduct which indeed is obnoxious to moral reprehension. But so mighty a form must trample down many an innocent flower, crush to pieces many an object in its path.[1]

In their case at least the end, of which they are not themselves fully conscious, justifies what would be otherwise objectionable means.

The apparently cynical nature of this conclusion, and of other parts of Hegel's doctrine, provokes the question whether a philosophy of history conceived on these lines can commend itself to moral reason. This is a point about which Hegel was himself quite properly sensitive, since for him as for others to demonstrate the rationality of history is to offer not only an intellectual explanation of the course of events, but a moral justification of it too. His main way of dealing, or attempting to deal, with the difficulty was by arguing that the true ethical unit is not the isolated individual but the 'moral organism', the state or society in which he was brought up, and that the claims of the latter must take precedence

1. *Lectures*, p. 34.

over those of the former. That the individual should perish for the good of the 'whole' does not strike him as morally outrageous. And if it is said that this involves the condonation of much that conscience condemns, his reply is that it is not self-evident that individual conscience is the highest court of appeal in these matters. Morality of conscience must in fact be replaced by an ethics based on the good of society, and if we adopt that standpoint and take a long view of events much that formerly seemed reprehensible will be seen to have its point.[1]

It may be added that it is in the light of this doctrine of 'social ethics' that Hegel's conception of freedom must be interpreted. It is certainly paradoxical that one whose political outlook was markedly anti-liberal should have made progress towards the realisation of freedom the goal of history. But by 'freedom' Hegel certainly did not mean mere absence of restraint: he vigorously repudiated the doctrine of natural rights. The difficult passage quoted on p. 140 shows his tendency to identify the free with the self-contained or self-sufficient, and he found this condition fulfilled not in the individual but in society. The freedom towards which history was moving was therefore the freedom of the community as a whole, whose requirements might (though they should not) strike individual citizens as externally imposed. It would, however, be wrong to press the antithesis of individual and society too far in Hegel's case, since a society which imposed a blank uniformity of behaviour on its members would have struck him as no better than one in which complete licence prevailed. Here as elsewhere his ideal was unity in diversity, a whole which realised itself in its members and was not to be thought of as separate from them.

§ 4. *Criticism of Hegel's theories*

The alarmingly contemporary ring of some of these opinions makes impartial criticism of the whole theory far from easy. Nevertheless, we must attempt to break through the fog of emotion with which the name of Hegel is now surrounded, and assess his views on their merits.

That Hegel himself made a substantial contribution to historical

1. Hegel developed these views on ethics at an early stage of his philosophical career: compare the essay on natural law contributed to Schelling's *Critical Journal of Philosophy* in 1802. Bradley drew extensively on this essay for his well-known discussion of 'My Station and its Duties' in *Ethical Studies* (1876).

studies is not in doubt. He was one of the first to write a history of philosophy, and his work in this connection had a powerful influence on his successors. Moreover, he shows throughout his writing a sense of the importance of the past for the understanding of the present which is entirely, or very largely, wanting in the thought of most eighteenth-century philosophers. If the Hegelian school had little or no effect on the development of the natural sciences during the nineteenth-century, it certainly gave a considerable fillip to the prosecution of social studies in that period.

But all this might have been true had Hegel written nothing on the subject of *philosophy* of history. Could it be claimed that his work in this field really did what it set out to do, namely, to make history intelligible as it had not been made intelligible before?

To judge by the reactions of professional historians the proper answer to this question would seem to be 'no'. For them the Hegelian philosophy of history, and for that matter speculative philosophies of history of all kinds, are of little or no interest. They look on such works, when they notice them at all, as imprudent attempts to impose a preconceived pattern on the actual course of events. The intelligibility which they themselves hope to find in history is not the sort of intelligibility these theories profess to offer.

It would, however, be unfair to take this opinion as settling the question without further ado, if only because Hegel himself to some extent anticipated the objection. As we have seen, he was anxious to distinguish his own undertaking in constructing a philosophy of history from that of everyday historians in establishing facts about the past, and would have expressed no surprise on being told that his aims made little appeal to them. On the other hand, he would certainly have repudiated the charge of seeking to impose a prearranged pattern on the actual course of events, maintaining that in his theory both *a priori* and empirical elements were in place, and that neither could supersede the other.

We must now try to estimate the adequacy of this defence. As regards the first point, it is surely successful. I have tried to stress throughout this chapter and the last the metaphysical and moral context within which speculative philosophy of history arose and was pursued. As we have seen, those engaged in these enquiries were concerned to divine the meaning or point or rationality behind the historical process as a whole, and they took up this question primarily because of its metaphysical relevance. And whatever else they may have intended by the vague terms 'meaning,' 'point,' etc., they certainly included a moral element in their connotation. In asking that history be shown to be intelligible, they were requiring that the contemplation of it should leave us morally satisfied, or at least not morally dissatisfied. This is obviously an aim quite foreign to the everyday historian, one which does not concern him *qua* historian at all.

Agreement on this point, however, would not remove for most working historians their suspicion of speculative philosophy of history. They would continue to regard a writer like Hegel with misgiving, feeling that there was something fundamentally wrong about his work, something alien to them quite apart from its moral and metaphysical twist. If asked to justify their misgivings they would probably again pin on the ambiguities of such words as 'intelligible.' 'The speculative philosophers of history,' we can imagine them saying, 'in seeking to show that history is an intelligible process, were not only making certain moral demands which do not concern us as historians; they were also professing to find in history a pattern or a rhythm which we as empirical enquirers are not able to detect. And their professions were in fact fraudulent, for they were only able to seem to do the trick at all by having recourse to considerations of abstract logic, considerations which may or may not have been valid in their proper sphere, but which were palpably without relevance to history itself.'

It is here that we come up against the central difficulties of a position like Hegel's. In a passage near the beginning of the lectures we read:

The only thought which philosophy brings with it to the contemplation of history is the simple thought of reason, that reason rules the world, and consequently that world history too is a rational process.[1]

But what is meant by 'a rational process' in this connection? We might agree to understand by such a process one which reason could explain or render intelligible; but then the question arises

1. *Dass es also auch in der Weltgeschichte vernünftig zugegangen sei:* Sibree translation, p. 9.

what it is to explain or render intelligible in history. Hegel and his critics appear to answer this question in different ways.

When a working historian talks of explaining or rendering intelligible an historical process he has in mind the procedures we have tried to analyse in a previous chapter—the 'colligating' of the events of which it consists by means of 'appropriate conceptions', the tracing in it of the working of general laws (whether those of psychology, sociology, etc., or the more familiar generalisations of common sense), and so on. If the process in question proves amenable to these procedures, and any others which reputable historians acknowledge, it is said to be explicable or intelligible. Should a questioner demand of the historian a further explanation once the procedures have been applied, he will simply get more of the same sort of thing: the origins of the process will be followed up further, its details more fully explored. In either case, the process will be said to be explained when the historian thinks himself in a position to construct what we previously called a significant narrative of the events in question.

Now when Hegel speaks of world history being a rational process, he is without doubt implying that it would be possible to construct a significant narrative (as opposed to an unconnected chronicle) of the events of which it consists; but he appears to be implying something more too, namely, that we could, in principle at any rate, say something not merely about the *causes* of what happened but about its *grounds* too. The suggestion that we explain an historical event when we sort out the different causal factors at work in it and estimate their importance would not content him: he wanted more explanation than that. And by 'more' in this connection he did not mean more explanation of the same kind as before. It was not the incompleteness of the story told by working historians which distressed him; it was its essential superficiality. To understand history in the proper sense we needed to get beyond the empirical standpoint altogether and approach it in quite another way.

The point will perhaps become clearer if we say that Hegel asks the question 'why?' about history in a sense different from that in which it is asked by working historians; or rather, that he asks 'why?' first in the straightforward historical sense or senses, and then in a further sense of his own. His doing so is to be connected

with his desire to penetrate behind the surface of historical phenomena to the reality which he has no doubt underlies them. This is
an achievement which we cannot expect of ordinary historians,
whose thought, in Hegelian jargon, 'moves at the level of the
understanding'; but it is one which falls very clearly in the province
of the philosopher, who has knowledge of the Idea at his disposal
to deepen his insight into facts.

But if this is what Hegel is after, how could he set about reaching
concrete results? So far as I can see, only two courses were open to
him. One was to try to deduce the details of history from the
categories of his logic. History would be a rational process in
Hegel's strong sense of the term if it could be shown to be entailed
by the abstract dialectic of the Idea. But, as we have seen, Hegel
himself was under no illusions about the possibility of carrying
such a deduction out. He therefore chose the alternative procedure,
which was to try to deduce not the details of history, but its outline
or skeleton plot, from purely philosophical premises.

Yet in choosing this alternative does he not lay himself open
to the very charge of *a priorism* he so vehemently seeks to repudiate?
And can he in fact produce a convincing answer to the charge? Is
it not clear that Hegel, on his own showing, knows a good deal
about the course history must take before he knows any historical
facts at all? He knows, for instance, that history must be the gradual
realisation of freedom; he even knows that this process must
complete itself in four distinct stages. If required, he will produce
philosophical proofs of these propositions. If this is not determining
the course of history apart from experience it is hard to know what
is.

Hegel might reply that the criticism is ill-conceived: that it
assumes the standpoint of the 'understanding' and fails to allow
for the special nature of philosophical reason, a faculty which is
not barely discursive but has intuitive powers too. But, we must
ask, how and where are these intuitive powers supposed to be
exercised? Is it suggested (as Herder, for example, might have
suggested) that the philosopher can discern the pattern to which
the empirical facts necessarily conform by scrutinising them
intelligently? If it is, then the question arises why working historians
cannot discern the pattern too. And if the reply is that they lack
acquaintance with the Hegelian logic, our comment must be that

that logic appears on this showing to be very much the *deus ex machina* its critics allege it to be.

There is a point in this connection which is worth further consideration. It is sometimes said that Hegel thought history a rational process because it culminated in the Prussian state in whose service he himself worked. The jibe is a cheap one and attributes to Hegel a provincialism which was not among his defects.[1] But a serious difficulty does lie behind the criticism. Hegel professes to tell us the plot of world history, and denies that his account of the matter is speculative in the bad sense of the term. But since history is an uncompleted process, how can its overall plot be empirically discovered? At the best we could say, with Kant, that experience *so far as it is available* confirms the interpretation of history which pure reason suggests. But if we did that we should be wise to put the goal of history in the future, and not regard it, as Hegel does, as culminating in the present. It is interesting to notice that he himself observes in one passage in the lectures that 'America is the land of the future, where, in the ages that lie before us, the burden of the world's history will reveal itself';[2] but how these ages are to be fitted into his scheme is not obvious.

It appears from this that the philosophy of history of Hegel is open to much the same objections as the philosophy of history of Kant; and indeed a cynic might say that it offers little more than an elaboration of the Kantian thesis, tricked out with a logical apparatus which makes it seem a great deal more profound. Hegel was certainly far more historically-minded than Kant, and the *Philosophy of History* is doubtless a more interesting work than any that Kant could have written on the subject; but the agreement in principle nevertheless remains. With both we find ourselves asking the question, what it is they suppose philosophy can contribute towards the understanding of history, and from neither do we get a satisfactory answer. If we concentrate on the direct effects of philosophy on history it seems that only two answers are possible, one so obvious as to be uninteresting, the other so wild as to be incredible. The first is that philosophy assures historians that if they try long and hard enough and are lucky enough to find

1. It should be noted that it is *die germanische Welt*, and not *die deutsche Welt* which constitutes the fourth stage of world history for him.
2. Sibree, p. 90.

the appropriate evidence they will in the end make sense of any historical situation. This is a 'truth' which all historians assume whether philosophy tells them it or not. The second is that if we look at the facts of history we shall see that they conform to a pattern which pure reason can work out independently of all experience. This is a suggestion which no genuine historian will believe. Neither Kant nor Hegel makes any third alternative clear.

To put the matter in this way is misleading, for it will inevitably be taken to imply that the whole search for a speculative philosophy of history was, from the theoretical point of view at least, a fantastic waste of time, on the same plane as, for example, efforts to foretell the future by measuring the Great Pyramid of Egypt; and this it most certainly was not. The sharp dichotomy, so acceptable to the simple-minded, between a useful activity called science carried on by sane men and a useless one called metaphysics carried on by knaves and fools is no more applicable here than it is elsewhere. The truth is that the speculations we have discussed did indirectly have a salutary effect on historical studies. By emphasising the need to present historical facts as a coherent and intelligible whole, they provoked dissatisfaction with the loose chronicles and empty moralising which still largely passed for history at the end of the eighteenth century, and so contributed substantially to the immense development of the subject during the nineteenth century, when the complex and critical study we know as history today finally took shape. And some of the ideas of the speculative philosophers of history, Hegel in particular, showed a depth of insight which later historians were to turn to good account. To give one instance only, the suggestion that, in studying the history of a given nation at a given time, we can find in the conception of a national spirit the connecting link between phenomena previously thought to be wholly separate, has proved a fertile source of empirical hypotheses, and may thus be said to have thrown real light on some dark places in history.

Our verdict on speculative philosophy of history must accordingly be a mixed one. In a way, we are forced to characterise it as utterly wrong-headed, since its programme amounts to an attempt to comprehend history from the outside; an attempt which, as Croce made clear long ago,[1] cannot have any appeal for working

1. *Theory and History of Historiography*, ch. IV.

historians. On the other hand, its most celebrated exponents certainly did make an important indirect contribution to the development of historical studies, as we have just tried to show. Whether there is any future in this type of philosophising is another question, dependent, it would seem, on what chance there is of anyone's producing a tenable moral justification of the course history has taken. On this we can remark only that though all previous attempts at such a justification—Kant's, for example, or Hegel's—have been bitterly criticised as instances of special pleading, this has not caused the abandonment of the general project. Philosophies of history of this sort continue to appear, and presumably will do for so long as evil is looked on as constituting a metaphysical problem.

8

SOME FURTHER WRITERS

In this final chapter I wish to comment briefly on three post-Hegelian writers whose theories have a certain affinity with those we have just discussed. The writers in question are Auguste Comte, Karl Marx and Arnold Toynbee. I do not claim that there is any very close relation between the three, and the sections which follow may accordingly seem somewhat disconnected. In that case the reader would do well to treat them as what in effect they are—a series of separate appendices to the second half of the book.

§ 1. *Comte and the positivist movement*

We have seen in Chapter 7 how Hegel regarded his philosophy as offering a synthesis of the abstract rationalism—the scientific outlook—of the Enlightenment and the Romantic philosophies of feeling which were developed in opposition to it. The breakdown of this synthesis, which followed in a remarkably short time the death of Hegel in 1831, led to a revival of the eighteenth-century trust in the omnicompetence of science, and in particular to a renewed demand for the application of scientific method to the study of human affairs. A new scientific philosophy was presented to the world under the title of Positivism, the explicit aim of which was to sort out genuine knowledge from mere superstition and idle guesswork, and to offer a means of putting subjects hitherto considered the province of metaphysical speculation on a sound scientific basis. The main architect of this philosophy, which was to have a considerable influence on nineteenth-century historiography, was the French writer Auguste Comte.

The Positivists and the speculative philosophers of history were at one in being dissatisfied with 'empirical' history, and in demanding that 'sense' be made of its fragmentary and unconnected facts. They differed in that whilst for a writer like Hegel the clue to history was to be found in the dialectic of the Idea, it lay for the Positivists in the discovery of the laws governing historical change, to be achieved by the elaboration of a new science which Comte called 'social dynamics'. The method to be followed to arrive at this result was professedly empirical: by studying different historical situations we were to hit on the general laws they exemplified. Yet just how much *a priori* theorising was mixed up with this empirical approach in the minds of the early Positivists is well illustrated by Comte's own case.

In 1822, when he was a young man of twenty-four, Comte made what seemed to him an epoch-making discovery: that the human mind, in its reflection on phenomena, naturally passes through three main phases. In the first or 'theological' phase it accounts for events by attributing them to the operation of controlling spirits or a single controlling spirit. In the second 'metaphysical' phase it replaces these spirits by abstract forces such as the force of gravity, and substitutes for God an impersonal Nature. In the third 'positive' or 'scientific' phase these fictions are abandoned, and men are content to record phenomena as they occur and to state the laws of their conjunction.

It was to this Law of the Three Stages, as it was called, that Comte had recourse when he set out to 'make sense' of the facts of history. History was intelligible, he believed, because in it we found the Law of the Three Stages writ large.

Accordingly we find Comte exhibiting the history of mankind (or rather that of Europe) as a progress in which the three stages are clearly traceable. First comes a long theological period, embracing, besides primitive savagery, the civilisations of Greece and Rome and the Middle Ages, and marked by a gradual transition from fetichism (animism) through polytheism to monotheism. Next with the Renaissance, the rise of science and the development of industry there followed the metaphysical stage: a period of criticism and negative thought, characterised by the breakdown of old institutions and culminating in the French Revolution. Lastly, we move to the Positivist era, only partially accomplished, which is to revive many of the features of medieval Christendom, with the important differences that it will rest on science, not on superstition, and that its pontiff will be not the Pope but Auguste Comte.

Extended comment on this is scarcely necessary. It is sufficient to remark that for Comte the course of history is at least as much determined by extra-historical considerations as it is for Hegel. Facts are forced into a rigid framework which is no less objectionable for being described as scientific rather than metaphysical, and which can be seen without difficulty to have been constructed to accommodate Comte's personal prejudices. The whole thing can have no more appeal to working historians than can speculative philosophies of history of the most metaphysical kind.

Despite this, the Positivist movement did, as we have already indicated, have a substantial influence on the development of historical studies during the century, though in a direction which made little appeal to its founder. This was in the impetus it gave to the examination of historical records and accumulation of historical data which was so marked a feature of nineteenth-century historiography. Impressed by the Positivist ideal of making history scientific, historians entered with zest on what was thought to be the first step towards its attainment, namely the ascertaining of precisely what occurred; and this resulted in the accumulation of rich collections of source material (for example, the collections of Latin and Greek inscriptions), of original texts critically edited and of other basic data which have been of immense value to their successors. Unfortunately for the Positivists, the rest of the programme, to deduce from the facts the general laws governing social change, had had little or no attraction for historians, who to this day have remained shut up in their own enquiries.[1]

The Positivist movement in history, as Croce has observed, was the obverse of the metaphysical movement. In each case something sound lay at its basis: the impulse to pass beyond a bare, 'unscientific' narrative of particular facts to a connected and intelligible account of them was a perfectly healthy one. Nor were

1. Professor Toynbee again constitutes an exception: see § 3 below.

the Positivists wrong, as we have argued earlier, in seeking to connect the understanding of history with a wider subject, the understanding of human nature in general. Where they were wrong was, first, in grossly underestimating the difficulties of putting the study of human nature on a scientific basis; secondly, in having altogether too simple a view of its connection with other studies, and thirdly, in thinking they could get historians to give up their own enquiries and transform themselves into social scientists. And they made the last mistake because, like the metaphysicians, they failed to see that history is an autonomous discipline, which certainly has its relations to other branches of learning, but is not therefore to be resolved into any of them.

§ 2. *Marx and historical materialism*

If the name of Comte is now largely forgotten, that of Marx arouses passions everywhere. Eager partisanship on the one hand, and violent antipathy on the other, prevent our making a sober assessment of his views, a task which is in any case far from easy because of the unsystematic character of Marx's writings and the fact that his aim was not so much to produce an intellectually watertight theory as provide an effective basis for political action. It was only incidentally that Marx was a philosopher in the sense in which, say, Kant and Hegel were philosophers. Yet his views do constitute an intellectual as well as a moral challenge, and could certainly not be left without mention in a work like this.

Here, however, I propose to attempt nothing like a full statement and criticism of Marx's theory of history. I shall try only to specify its relations to other views current at the time, and to examine the general character of its assertions, with the object of showing that the final decision for or against it cannot be taken by philosophers.

Any discussion of Marx, however brief, must begin by considering his relation to Hegel. Marx was born in 1818, when Hegel was at the height of his powers, and entered the University of Berlin in 1836, when controversies on the merits of the Hegelian philosophy were still raging fiercely. And however much he came later to differ from the Hegelian point of view it remains true that certain elements of Hegelianism took a permanent hold on his thought, which cannot be understood without reference to them. We shall mention two Hegelian doctrines which are of special importance for Marx's theory of history. First, the dialectic. Here we need to distinguish. Marx objected from the first to the idealist or (if the term is preferred) rationalist character of Hegelian metaphysics, i.e. to the view that the universe is, properly speaking, the self-expression of Spirit. Such an account struck him as wholly unplausible: Hegel, he said, had precisely inverted the true state of the facts, for (as science showed) Matter preceded Spirit, not Spirit Matter.[1] Yet this rejection of the priority of Spirit was *not* accompanied (even if it ought to have been) by a rejection of the dialectic: Marx was as insistent on dialectic as Hegel. Reality might not be the self-expression of Spirit, but relations of the dialectical pattern were all the same traceable everywhere in the facts. Dialectic was important not because it answered to the nature of thought, but because it answered to the nature of things.

Secondly, Marx took over from Hegel the view that the different aspects of a society's life at any one time are organically related, though he gave it a peculiar twist of his own. Hegel, as we saw, was anxious to maintain that there was constant interaction between, e.g., the political, economic and cultural life of a nation at any one time; he explained the interaction by postulating a national spirit or genius which expressed itself in these diverse fields. Here again Marx adopted Hegel's conclusion without accepting his premises. The organic connection of which Hegel spoke was, in his view, a real one, but we had no need to invoke the mysteries of a national spirit to account for it. It was explained far more cogently if we noticed that one aspect of social life, namely the economic aspect, was of such importance that it tended to be reflected in all the rest, so that it was in economic terms that all states of affairs must finally be understood.

These two Hegelian doctrines, taken in the way Marx took them, constitute the essentials of the Marxist theory of history. To make an instructive analysis of the situation in any field of social life at any one time we must refer to the economic conditions prevailing in the society; and to understand why those conditions are what they are we must consider their dialectical development. We must see how the economic organisation or class structure of

1. In metaphysics Marx was not a simple materialist, but a supporter of the theory of emergent evolution, according to which conscious life has developed from conditions which were at first wholly material.

a society is evolved in response to the need to solve a certain production problem, itself set by the state of the forces of production available to the society; and observe how developments in the forces of production put the existing economic organisation—the 'relations of production'—out of date, so giving rise to the need for fundamental social change.

We can, if we like, represent Marx's philosophy of history as an amended version of Hegel's, and certainly the two have superficially a good deal in common. Hegel had portrayed history as a dialectical progress towards the realisation of freedom, alleged to have been achieved in some degree in the Western civilisation of his own day. In this progress different nations come successively to the fore, each making its contribution to the ultimate end. Marx too thought of history as a dialectical progress towards a morally desirable goal, the classless communist society, which would in fact be a genuinely free society; though he put the attainment of that happy state of affairs in the not too distant future rather than the present. And the chief actors in the drama of history were in his view not peoples or nations but economic classes; though here again each had its special contribution to make.

On this interpretation Marx is taken as very much the product of his time, inspired with the contemporary urge to 'make sense' of history, and dominated by the ethical preoccupations which gave rise to the speculative philosophies we have examined. That it is not a wholly false interpretation I hope to have shown: there is, in this matter, a genuine continuity between Marx and his predecessors. It is none the less a very misleading one, if put forward as anything like a complete account of the subject.

For if Marx is without doubt a follower of Hegel's in important respects, he also has much in common with a very different tradition of thought. I refer to the scientific tradition of the eighteenth-century Encyclopaedists, represented in practical affairs by the Benthamites, in the sphere of theory by Comte and the Positivists. Marx himself had nothing but contempt for both these groups, but this should not be allowed to disguise his affinities (I do not say his indebtedness) to them. Like Comte, he hoped to put the study of history on a scientific basis, which for him too meant explaining historical phenomena in terms which were other than mystical and metaphysical. And he was eager to do this because, like Bentham,

he was imbued with a passion for practical reform, embodied in
his well-known comment (which conveniently forgets Bentham)
that 'previous philosophers have sought only to understand the
world; the point is, however, to change it.'

These considerations suggest another way of looking at Marx's
theory of history. Instead of regarding it as yet another philosophy
of the speculative type, in which an attempt is made to find unity
and intelligibility in the historical process as a whole, we can treat
it rather as a theory of historical interpretation, concerned with the
elucidation of particular situations. On this view it can be represented as recommending to historians a way of dealing with any
events they may be called on to explain. 'To understand any
process of change in history', we may take Marx as saying, 'have
an eye to the economic background against which the change took
place, and analyse that background by means of the concepts my
theory provides. Only in this way will the process become intelligible, for only in this way will you get down to fundamental
questions.'

This interpretation of the theory certainly corresponds to Marx's
own attitude to it. His interests being overwhelmingly practical,
he needed the theory not so much for its speculative content as
for its predictive properties. He wanted to find his way through
the thicket of contemporary events, to make sense not of history
as a whole but of what was happening at the time and what had
happened in the comparatively recent past. That the theory should
work for the period of modern European history from the rise of
capitalism onwards was of infinitely more importance to him than
that it might be difficult to apply to remote times and peoples.
Had anyone shown that it could *not* be applied to some such remote
period, Marx, having a strong speculative streak in him, would
certainly have been piqued; but he could all the same have accepted
the point with equanimity so long as his theory's effectiveness for
recent history remained unchallenged.

It may be added that the interest shown in Marxism by working
historians is also to be connected with the theory's serving as a
guide to the interpretation of particular historical situations, a sort
of recipe for producing empirical hypotheses. Unlike his predecessors, Marx had produced something which could, according to
the professions of its author, be turned to account in actual historical

work; and the professions were clearly not wholly false. Hence the attitude of the average historian towards the Marxist theory, whatever the view taken of its ultimate tenability, has been quite different from the corresponding attitude to the writers we discussed earlier; and the reason is that Marx's theory has, whilst theirs have not,[1] this empirical side to it.

We must now ask what light philosophers can be expected to throw on the truth or falsity of Marx's views. That they can make some useful comments on them I do not wish to deny. For, after all, Marx professes, on the interpretation we have put forward, to be making a *reasoned* recommendation to historians; in his own language, his theory differs from other views of the same general sort (for example, other versions of historical materialism) in having a 'scientific' basis. And this scientific basis is certainly worth philosophical scrutiny, for the precise character of the propositions of which it consists is by no means clear.

By way of illustration, let us briefly consider the function of dialectic in Marx's account. We have seen how Marx accepted the Hegelian dialectic whilst rejecting the philosophical arguments with which Hegel had supported it. That thought should proceed dialectically rested in his view on there being dialectical connections in things; and that there were such connections, and indeed that they were ubiquitous, struck him as an evident fact. But we must ask what all this implies for the logical basis of Marx's theory. What is the status in the Marxist account of the proposition that all things are dialectically connected? Hegel could hold it to be a necessary truth, demonstrable by reason, since he believed that facts reflect the dialectical character of thought, itself guaranteed by reason's insight into its own nature. But Marx, who had abandoned these idealist doctrines, could make no such claim. All he could say, to be consistent with himself, was that we know from experience that things are dialectically connected, i.e. that the proposition in question is an empirical truth. Yet to have to admit this is distinctly awkward for him, since it leaves open the possibility that situations may turn up to which the dialectical scheme will not apply, when his whole attitude is based on the exclusion of this possibility.

These remarks will perhaps suffice to bring out an important

1. Or do not appear to have. But compare the remarks on Hegel on p. 149 above.

ambiguity in the Marxist theory. The dialectic, as we have seen, is a vital constituent of that theory; any Marxist asked to defend his approach to history would fall back on it sooner or later. But the question arises whether it will bear the weight Marx puts upon it. If it rests entirely on past experience it will certainly not: however well-established the generalisation that things are dialectically connected, no such generalisation can be taken as without question prescriptive to all future experience. And if Marx says that it is an *a priori* proposition, not an empirical truth, then he must attempt a philosophical justification of it; and this he entirely fails to do.

There are other elements in the Marxist theory to which philosophers could profitably give their attention: the sense in which the forces of production are alleged to 'develop' (a matter of major importance for Marx) is one example, that in which the different aspects of social life are held to form an organic whole despite the overwhelming predominance of one constituent, another. I think it is possible to show that Marx runs into difficulties, or at least is unclear, over both of these points, though I do not propose to make the attempt here.

Yet it remains true that whatever damage philosophical criticism can do to the Marxist theory, it cannot overthrow it altogether. The reason for this should not be difficult to see. The theory (at least on our interpretation of it) recommends to historians a procedure for dealing with empirical situations; and the ultimate test of it must be whether it is in fact a fruitful procedure. This is something on which no *a priori* pronouncement can be made: it can be decided only by actually following the recommendation and seeing what happens. Hence the final decision for or against the Marxist approach to history must lie with those historians who try to follow it. We must ask them if it proves an illuminating approach, if its recommendations are sufficiently specific to be useful, if certain obvious unplausibilities about it (difficulties about great men, national feeling, etc.) can be satisfactorily met. But these are questions which non-historians cannot hope to answer for themselves. In the last resort, the proof of the Marxist pudding is in the eating, and it is not philosophers whom Marx invites to sample his dish.

It was for this reason that I suggested in my introductory chapter (p. 28 above) that the main contribution Marx had to make to the understanding of history might not have been made to philosophy of history, properly speaking, at all. Marx's theory certainly does involve assumptions which philosophers can usefully examine: it would indeed be odd if this were not so when we remember the time at which he lived and the background against which he wrote. But even if it could be shown that he was wrong in making every one of these assumptions, that would not destroy the validity of the theory; it would only discredit the reasons Marx gave for it. It might, after all, be the case that economic causes were fundamental for the understanding of all historical situations even if everything Marx alleged in support of that view was false.

§ 3. *Toynbee's study of history*

It remains to say something of a modern writer on universal history whose work has been the subject of very wide interest and discussion. I refer to Professor A. J. Toynbee, whose ten-volume *Study of History* began to appear in 1934 and was completed twenty years later.[1]

The first difficulty with Toynbee is to know how to take his work. Originally, he appeared to have in mind nothing more than a comparative study of the rise, growth and declines of civilisations. He began by arguing that a civilisation is the sole intelligible unit of historical study, went on to identify twenty-one civilisations past and present, and proceeded to isolate what he took to be recurring features in their histories. His attitude here was, according to his own declaration, strictly empirical; he was anxious, in particular, to contrast himself in this respect with the German writer Oswald Spengler, whose *Decline of the West* (1918), though obviously similar in its aims, struck him as the work of a 'philosopher-hierophant'. It soon emerged, however, that Toynbee's conception of empirical methods was somewhat idiosyncratic. Certainly he had a wide, indeed an encyclopaedic, knowledge of historical facts, and was anxious throughout to adduce evidence in support of his theories. But he held to these with a conviction which was hardly dispassionate (his work from the first had an intensely personal air), and even in the first volume supported them by references to mythological and poetic ideas which made more

---

1. [Vols. VII–X appeared in 1954 and complete the work proper. Vol. XI is an historical atlas and gazetteer. Vol. XII, which came out in 1961, contains a series of afterthoughts and replies to critics, both developed at great length. I discuss its philosophical aspects in 'Toynbee Reconsidered,' *Philosophy*, 1963.]

sober enquirers uneasy. Nor did his detailed interpretations of particular historical situations always find favour with experts in those fields: it was commonly said that he had, to a greater or less extent, distorted the facts to suit his theories. If Toynbee's *Study* was thus originally conceived on lines which recall the aspirations of Comte, it was certainly not carried out in a straightforwardly scientific manner.

To say this is not necessarily to condemn Toynbee out of hand, for there have been other writers in this field whose procedures have been individual but who have none the less achieved striking results. One is Spengler himself, whose highly impressionistic study, marred as it is by being over-schematic and careless of historical detail, still finds many readers; another is the early eighteenth-century Italian philosopher Giambattista Vico. Toynbee resembles Vico in several important respects[1]: in wanting to trace what Vico calls an 'ideal human history,' a sort of life-cycle through which all advanced societies must pass; in approaching his problem by meditating carefully on a single case, the history of the ancient classical world; finally, in relying on bold analogical argument and sources not much considered by more conventional enquirers to further his highly imaginative conclusions. Personally, I very much doubt whether Toynbee has anything like the genius of Vico, but at least Vico's case shows that, in dealing with such a wide and amorphous subject-matter, power of insight and fertility of hypothesis can be more important factors than simple scientific accuracy. If Toynbee sometimes gets his facts wrong, we ought not to insist on that too pedantically, for in this sphere at least a man can be wrong in detail and sound in essentials.

Whether this defence succeeds or not, it is clear that Toynbee could not rely on it exclusively. I say this because of the remarkable shift in the author's interest which became evident in the later volumes of his work. At the beginning, as I have already pointed out, his approach was, broadly, that of a sociologist; he seemed to be undertaking an empirical enquiry into the factors governing the rise and decline of civilisations. In the final volumes, however, the role for which he has cast himself is very much more that of a prophet. We find him here, in fact, meditating on the meaning

1. But oddly enough does not mention him in *A Study of History*. [Vico is referred to several times in vol. XII, for which see the preceding note.]

F

of history in a way which closely recalls that followed by the speculative philosophers of history whose work we have analysed above: like them, the question he puts is whether history as a whole makes sense, and like them he assumes that an affirmative answer to this question can be given only if there is good reason to suppose that it is proceeding to a morally satisfactory goal. Toynbee has persuaded himself that he can give this answer because he thinks he has discovered the 'raison d'être,' to use his own term,[1] behind the many disasters that have overtaken civilised men in the past: the purpose of these catastrophes was, apparently, to prepare for a coming synthesis of the four 'higher religions', a synthesis which still lies in the future, but in anticipation of which Toynbee has composed, in the very last pages of his *Study*,[2] a number of specimen prayers.

In moving thus from sociology to metaphysics Toynbee is by no means alone among those who have concerned themselves with patterns and laws in history. Vico made the same transition when he sought to reconcile his doctrine of recurring cycles with an orthodox Christian belief in Providence; Herder (whom Toynbee recalls in other respects as well, for example in his predilection for understanding historical processes in terms which are drawn from biology) also has a quasi-scientific and a more frankly speculative side to his thought. It is perhaps not altogether surprising that those who fish in these waters should come up with some strange catches. What is surprising is that a modern fisherman should have so little awareness of the experiences of his predecessors and be so painfully unconscious of the diverse character, to say nothing of the difficulties, of what he is attempting. Any hope that Toynbee has of persuading us that he is producing important new truths at the end of his mammoth work must rest on a clear recognition of the character of what is there asserted; but, despite much criticism, Toynbee himself remains apparently quite unaware of the point.

His confusion is, indeed, worse than has so far been indicated, for he not only appears to see no difference between discovering patterns in history and plotting the course of history as a whole: he identifies both with doing history *sans phrase*. The author of

1. *A Study of History*, VII, 422.
2. op. cit., X, 143–4.

A Study of History persistently presents himself to his public as an *historian*, a simple student of the past who looks at what happened and writes down obvious facts. In truth, however, no description could be less appropriate. Toynbee was not an historian at the beginning of his work when he sought to discover the laws governing historical change, for his interest then was not in particular events but in repeated patterns. To enquire into historical laws is not identical with doing history in the ordinary sense, but rather presupposes it: unless ordinary history first exists, no such enquiry can be undertaken. Toynbee perhaps fails to notice this extremely obvious point because there are fields, such as the history of Sparta, in which he has himself made historical contributions; but it becomes crystal-clear when we observe his treatment of, say, the civilisations of Central and South America, where his dependence on results established by firsthand students of those cultures is patent. Nor are the questions Toynbee raises at the end of his book historical questions proper. True, he is there concerned with the course of individual events, but not as historians are. The latter confine themselves to the discovery and understanding of what went on in the past; in so far as they aim at 'making sense' of something, it is of a set of events limited both in space and time and now over and done with. Toynbee, by contrast, not only takes all history as his province; he extends his enquiry from the past to the future and purports to pronounce on 'the prospects of western civilisation'. No doubt it is this extension which has brought Toynbee's book so much attention, to the chagrin of genuine historians whose readers wonder why their work cannot have the same exciting qualities; but this too is the result of confusion, not a reason for overlooking it.

Not only is Toynbee in the *Study* not an historian[1]; he has everything to gain from recognising the fact, for much of the abuse which has been poured on his book has come from historically minded critics who were as unclear about what he was attempting as he was himself. Why then is he so reluctant to give up the description? Perhaps the answer to this is to be found in the autobiographical account of the genesis of his work which Toynbee has inserted in vol. X (especially pp. 91–8). It becomes clear from

1. This explains why his work is irrelevant to the questions about the relationship of history and the sciences raised in Chapters 2 and 3 above.

this, not only that Toynbee sees himself as in some way doing over again the work of Gibbon, but also that his original intention amounted to nothing more than to write a comparative history of the declines of Greco-Roman and western civilisations. Certainly his horizon began to expand rapidly as he went into the project: from this 'originally binocular view of history'[1] he moved quickly to a vision which was distinctly multiocular, with the result that before very long he was writing not only the decline and fall of the Roman Empire but the decline and fall of every empire under the sun, with accounts of their rises thrown in for good measure. Here he had passed, as we have argued above, outside the range of any sort of history: the mantle of Gibbon had been exchanged for that of Comte. But the fact that the transition was made in stages, and that the question of the true causes of the fall of the ancient classical world remained one of his chief preoccupations, has served, so far at least, to conceal its existence from this otherwise acute 'post-modern western student of history'.

Will anyone read *A Study of History* in fifty years time? The book is so much a product of its author's not always very interesting personal opinions and prejudices and is, in its later parts at least, so extraordinarily ill-written that I doubt whether many will. In this respect it looks as if Toynbee will share the fate of Herbert Spencer, another synthetic philosopher of large pretensions. Yet his ideas may, even so, have their effect. If his detailed contribution to the comparative study of civilisations turns out in the end not to be of great significance—as critics have pointed out, many of his leading ideas, such as challenge and response, withdrawal and return, are disappointingly imprecise—that will not take away from the achievement of having sketched the idea and taken the initial steps in carrying it out. Toynbee is no doubt less of a pioneer than he seems to imagine, but he deserves credit for pioneering all the same. His results here are, in any case, likely in my view to prove more substantial than anything he has accomplished as a speculative philosopher of history, where the advantages of his vivid imagination can scarcely outweigh the disadvantage of having a singularly muddled intellect. Perhaps his main service, however, will be to history itself, in so far as his work may be expected to break down the parochialism of professional historians by drawing

1. op. cit., X, 97.

attention to whole subjects of study which are commonly ignored. Whatever is said about Toynbee, at least he thinks of the past as something genuinely worth knowing about, not merely as a source of material on which to exercise a series of technical skills. Professional historians are often right to criticise him, but many of them could do with some of his largeness of mind.

ADDITIONAL ESSAYS

(A)

THE LIMITS OF SCIENTIFIC HISTORY

The question I propose to discuss is the ancient one of whether history is, or can be, a science. This is a topic on which much has been written, but about which, as it seems to me, a good deal of confusion persists. I shall approach it now by commenting on certain aspects of the controversy about scientific history carried on by the Cambridge historians J. B. Bury and G. M. Trevelyan in the early years of the present century. I choose this statement of the issues, despite its relative antiquity, because I find that in it the main points to be decided emerge with fair clarity. I also think it important that historians should see that the problems involved are not the invention of meddlesome philosophers, but arise naturally out of intelligent reflection on their subject. And if any historian wants to assure me that history has moved on since 1903, I will admit that it has, but ask leave to doubt whether the distance travelled is sufficient to put the Bury-Trevelyan controversy out of court. A glance at Professor Trevor-Roper's inaugural lecture, *History, Professional and Lay* (Oxford, 1958), would certainly suggest that it is not.[1]

Let me begin then by asking what Bury meant by his celebrated declaration that 'history is a science, no less and no more'. I take it first as being clear that Bury had no intention of claiming that history issues, or might issue, in general conclusions, and I shall dismiss that possibility from consideration here. The main points

1. For Bury's views see his inaugural lecture 'The Science of History', reprinted in his *Selected Essays* (1927). Trevelyan's answer, 'Clio, a Muse', was first printed in the *Independent Review*, December 1903. I should make clear that I discuss the views of these writers only so far as they are expressed in the above works.

he had in mind seem to me to be these. First, that thanks to the enormous advances in the techniques for finding and exploiting historical evidence made in the three generations before his own, historians were at last in a position to claim scientific status for their results, i.e. to claim ability to make definitively true statements about the past. And second, that when he had arrived at results of that kind, the historian had finished his task: his concern was with the truth and nothing but the truth. The first point explains why Bury said that history is 'no less' than a science, the second why he added that it is 'no more' than one. As the context makes abundantly clear, Bury was protesting here against the assumption, which he attributed to the great amateur historians of the past, that history ought to be something more than a bare account of what truly happened: it should be, if not exactly a philosophical meditation on the meaning of the events in question, at least a dramatic and literary presentation of them, in which the personal qualities and outlook of the historian concerned were well in evidence. Against that Bury wanted to say that the time had come to divorce history from literature and to abstract from the personality of the historian. The business of history was solely to discover the truth, and the discovery of truth was an enterprise which could best be carried on co-operatively, in history as in other sciences.

   In putting these points forward Bury relied primarily on an argument from fact. It just was the case that in the second half of the nineteenth century historical studies had been transformed, and history developed from an affair for amateurs into a professional discipline with exacting standards of its own. In becoming an academic subject (though Bury himself did not emphasise this side of the matter) history had changed its status, much as archaeology has in the course of the present century. It was no longer an affair of guesswork, but a field in which certain knowledge was arrived at daily. Yet for all this optimism, Bury was under no illusions about the incomplete character of the revolution he proclaimed. Even in Germany, its home, the revolution was far from complete, as the existence of diverse schools of historians showed. And while it might be true that historians had taken the all-important step of realising that we must see all periods of the past *sub specie perennitatis*, thus abandoning the provincialism of outlook which had marred the work of their predecessors, they were clearly far from building up the agreed picture of past events which must, on Bury's view of the matter, be their eventual goal. Indeed, Bury himself spoke of the position as he saw it with profound modesty: the best he could offer his fellow-workers in the field of historical scholarship was that they should proceed with their 'patient drudgery' and 'microscopic research' as an act of faith—'in the faith' (to quote his own words) 'that a complete assemblage of the smallest facts of human history will tell in the end'.[1]

Bury's declaration that history is a science might thus have been more properly expressed as a claim, the claim that it is on the way to becoming one. But we come here to an important ambiguity of which Bury himself was to all appearances unaware. As already noted, the consideration which moved him most was the evident fact that history in his time, in contrast to history, say, a century before, was in a position to establish some conclusions with certainty. History was like a science in having developed techniques which were not the peculiar possession of a few gifted individuals, but could be shared and practised by intelligent men generally, given proper training; and when these techniques were applied, the results achieved were such that, in favourable cases at any rate, there could no longer be serious dispute about their acceptability. This meant, as I said before, that historians were able to reach definitive truths about the past. But it is one thing to arrive at definitive *truths*, another at definitive *truth*. In fact all that Bury was justified in maintaining, on the strength of the facts to which he pointed, was that historians have reliable and agreed procedures for answering questions about what in particular occurred: they know how to settle some questions definitively, in a way which makes it pointless to pursue them further. Bury simply assumed that, if only this process were carried further, if only we went on patiently getting bits of the picture right, an authentic reconstruction of the whole would emerge, and we should pass painlessly from knowing truths about the past to knowing *the* truth. Despite the disclaimers with which he surrounded it, the assumption was to say the least naïve.

Trevelyan was on to this point, in a confused sort of way, when he argued against Bury that it was only in the matter of establishing basic facts that history could be scientific. Historians, in Trevelyan's

1. *Selected Essays*, p. 17.

view, had not only to establish facts; they had also to discover their causes or interpret them. Now I think that we can set aside this question of discovering causes at once, on the ground that if it can be scientifically determined that so-and-so occurred, it can also be scientifically determined that it had such-and-such effects[1]; saying what the facts were and seeing their interconnections, though sometimes distinct, are not really disparate operations. But 'interpretation' is another matter. I mean by this by no means perspicuous term the activity in which at any rate some historians engage of giving a picture of an age, or a period of historical development, as a whole; as I see the matter, it is pictures of this sort which laymen expect professional historians to provide. And I think it is at any rate plausible to contend, as Trevelyan appeared to do, that putting a construction on the facts (which is what making such a picture involves) is evidently different, and calls for different abilities, from establishing particular happenings. It is because he does not even see that there might be a problem here that Bury is so unconvincing. However badly Trevelyan argued against him, at least he had revealed an important gap in Bury's case.

What exactly that gap is I hope to indicate in the sequel. Meantime, let me call attention to another element in Trevelyan's criticism of Bury which clearly connects with the subject just discussed, namely his rejection of the view that history is no more than a science. It is scarcely surprising that the grand-nephew of Macaulay thought nothing of the suggestion that the whole, and sole, task of history was to reveal the truth about the past, entirely for its own sake. But historians ought not to let the comfortable reflection that Trevelyan had a sort of vested interest here blind them to the essential reasonableness of his case on this point. If we are to judge by history as it was at the beginning of this century, and indeed still is, Trevelyan was entirely right to maintain that the subject has quite other sides to it than those that Bury recognised. The word 'history' may suggest to the professional student who spends his days in the British Museum or the Record Office accumulating results which he hopes to publish in learned periodicals for the benefit of his fellow scholars, little more than a series of intriguing intellectual puzzles, worthy of attention for their own sake; but to a wider public it has always meant something more. Whether the

1. For a modification of this somewhat optimistic view, see the following essay.

professional historian likes it or not, the approach of the plain man (I mean the intelligent plain man) to history is by no means disinterested: he studies the past not just out of idle curiosity (though this can on occasion be his motive), but because he finds a knowledge of it indispensable if he is to make a balanced assessment of his own times. The pictures which historians paint of past ages (G. M. Young's essay on early Victorian England would be an obvious example) can thus play a powerful and important part in general education. And this point can be made without our having to agree that the historians who write the sort of history here in question are untrue to their profession. Their view of the past may be less innocent than they think (I shall have more to say about this), but this does not mean that it must be coloured by prejudice. Prejudiced history, history written to advance a cause, does have its effect on the layman, but so does reputable history too.

Now it is of course open to the professional historian to say at this point that what the layman makes of history is neither here nor there: only those trained in the subject know what it really is. So far as I can judge from the outside, this has in fact been the reaction of most British working historians to Trevelyan's arguments about the wider aspects of history. To most of my former historical colleagues in Oxford, for instance, history is a specialist activity, an affair of greater and greater detail, subtle, exacting, in a real sense esoteric; it is emphatically not an attempt to tell the story of mankind to the average intelligent man. Doubtless if you pressed him you could get even an Oxford historian to admit that it was not the whole object of his activity to solve particular puzzles; there would still be the unexpressed hope that solving such puzzles would, in Bury's phrase, 'tell in the end', by enabling some more synoptic thinker to construct a more general picture, though a picture whose generality was still somewhat limited, a picture of the state of the Church in 1250, for instance, rather than a general picture of the Middle Ages. But for many working historians such a consummation, if desirable, is also remote: general surveys must be left to writers of textbooks, who can plead pedagogical exigency in their defence, and to a few men of genius. Meantime the average modest student of history (and historians are mostly modest, too much so in my opinion) will not regard it as a good reason for taking up an historical topic that it excites strong contemporary interest. Thus the history of the nineteenth century, which stirs our passions because it is so near to us and because the men of that time were at once so like and so unlike ourselves, will be less suitable for serious study than the history of the fourteenth, which we can regard with comparative equanimity. All periods are equally near to God, as Ranke told us, but some, those we should normally care about relatively little, enjoy Ranke's successors' particular favour.

I am aware that these remarks may well strike professional historians as unfair. I know that the concentration on medieval history which was for so long the central feature of British historical teaching might be justified on the ground that nowhere else (except perhaps in ancient history?) can students be introduced more effectively to the fundamental historical processes of discovering and exploiting evidence. I know too that some medievalists would argue that we cannot hope to understand what the world is today without an intimate knowledge of medieval times; though I must add that in my ignorance I remain sceptical on this point, regarding it as obvious that you would find out more about the modern world if you studied the political and social developments of the eighteenth and nineteenth centuries than if you went back to the twelfth and thirteenth. Setting these points aside, however, I find it difficult to take with due seriousness the conception of the nature and tasks of history to which so many professional historians apparently subscribe. That history, of all subjects, should be something which only scholars can practise and hope to understand; that it should be pursued not merely in an impartial spirit, but in deliberate abstraction from any interest which its results might have; that the personalities of those engaging in it should count for nothing, except in the sense that it is these particular persons and not others who think, as individual natural scientists think, of fruitful or abortive hypotheses—these propositions, so far from being self-evident, seem to me in every case open to question. As for the associated thesis that it does not matter what the historian studies so long as he genuinely uncovers new knowledge, I do not believe that you have to be a *Lucky Jim* type of historian to see it for the nonsense that it is. I am glad to be confirmed in some of these heresies by Professor Trevor-Roper, whose argument about the connexion between history and a lay public seems to me unanswerable, and who is, I think, right to insist that history is, in an important respect, a humane discipline rather than a science. If it is any consolation to historians, let me add that there has been a parallel misconception of their subject in the last fifty years by philosophers, who have also imagined themselves to be a species of scientist, and have thus produced the sort of analytic philosophy which is all I can practise myself, instead of the construction and criticism of metaphysical views which is what the public really wants from them.

I must now try to explain, in a somewhat less rhetorical way, why I think it a mistake to describe history as a science 'no less and no more'. It may help if I say at once that, for the purposes of this essay, I am prepared to accept everything Bury says about historians having developed reliable techniques for establishing particular facts. If to say that history is a science is only to call attention to those techniques and maintain that they can be used to good effect, I have no wish to dispute the proposition. But it seems to me that those who put it forward have usually meant a good deal more by it.

One thing they have meant is that history is, ideally at any rate, a body of established truth, which holds without distinction of persons. This strikes me as at once true and untrue. It is true in so far as the facts which an historian recites are, if properly authenticated, in no sense his personal possession, but are rather something to which any reasonable person must give his assent if he investigated them. That the French Revolution broke out in 1789 is not a truth for Frenchmen as opposed to Englishmen, or a truth for those who approve of the Revolution but not for those who detest it: it just is, whether we like it or not, a fact. But when we turn from the individual facts to the whole they constitute, it is less easy to abstract from personal considerations, as we can see by asking whether the French Revolution is the same thing for Frenchmen and non-Frenchmen, or among Frenchmen whether it is the same thing for men of the Left and men of the Right.

These questions are, of course, radically ambiguous, since what the French Revolution *is* might be taken to cover what it *means* to different individuals, which would in turn include what it *suggests* to them, how they *feel* about it, and so on. I do not wish to beg the question by introducing this kind of consideration, which professional historians might consider entirely irrelevant. Instead I should like to concentrate on what the historian would call the French Revolution as it was in itself. It seems to me that there are important differences, insufficiently appreciated by the advocates of scientific history, between writing about a thing like the French Revolution and writing about a topic in natural science.

There is, first of all, the fact that the historian of the French Revolution is a man who has a story to tell, that he is himself a particular person telling it and that he necessarily does his work with at any rate a general kind of audience in mind. The way someone tells a story depends not merely on what he has to tell; it depends also, in respects with which we are all familiar, on his own interests and preconceptions and those of the persons for whose benefit he is telling it. This does not mean that stories are irretrievably biased; it means only that every story contains an account of the facts as seen from a particular point of view. There is, if we like to use a dangerous term, a subjective component to every story; or to put the point less misleadingly, every narrative is someone's narrative, told, we may add, to some other party. To treat a narrative without reference to narrator or audience is to leave something of real importance out of account.

Before developing this point further I should like to consider two objections which would challenge its relevance to our present subject. The first is the objection that not all history takes the form of narrative. In addition to the history which takes you through the various stages of a particular development, there is the sort of history which, as it were, centres round a point and offers you a kind of orderly picture, or which covers the same ground over and over again from many angles. Halévy's *History of the English People in 1815* and Tocqueville's *Democracy in America* would be examples. Social history in particular readily takes this form. I am not, however, in the least troubled by the existence of analytic histories of this sort, since it seems to me plain that they, like simple narratives, are written from a particular over-all point of view. In them too what is picked out for emphasis depends not only on the nature of the material to be dealt with (though of course it does partly and importantly depend upon that), but also on the interests and outlook of the person making the survey and on those of the persons for whom he is writing. If we cannot strictly speak of a 'narrator' here, some more generic term such as 'expositor' will certainly be in place.

A second objection might question the implied contrast between history and natural science with which I am working. It might be said, in the first place, that you could, if you chose, present scientific results in quasi-historical form. Instead of a chapter in *The Principles of Mechanics*, for example, you might have 'A Day in the Life of a perfectly round Ball, rolling down a perfectly smooth inclined Plane'. Plato in his account of the decline of the soul and the state in Books VIII and IX of the *Republic* contrived in effect to write up sociological results in this way.[1] And of course this sort of thing is perfectly possible in other sciences, though to carry it out seriously might be cumbersome as well as precious. I think, even so, that the narrative form in cases of this kind is really no more than a peda-gogical device, enabling the writer to gain an entry to the minds of his readers by linking up his material with familiar experiences: the fact that we find it resorted to only in primers and school texts would seem to confirm this. And if it were said that a more serious comparison could be made between scientific works which set out the sum of knowledge on some particular topic and the analytic histories referred to above, I should again want to say that there is the all-important difference that whereas in the former the content is primarily determined by the subject-matter (or rather by what we know of it), quite different factors also enter into the latter. The fact that you can translate scientific textbooks from one language to another and put them to immediate use, when the operation is a far more delicate one in the case of works of history, clearly has a bearing on this point.

But what, after all, is it that comes into history when we recognise the indispensability of the expositor? Some people speak as if it were the factor of *selection*. According to this argument, history is, roughly, the story of the past as seen by a particular individual, who makes his selection among the multitude of past happenings according to his peculiar preconceptions. I have known historians so embarrassed by this argument that they have taken the heroic course of maintaining that history proper is not selective at all:

1. For this see my paper 'Plato and the Philosophy of History' in *History and Theory*, vol. II (1962).

ideally it aims at the resurrection of the entire past of man. It ought, however, to be obvious that the fact that history selects by no means implies that it is subjective in any bad sense. If a narrative is condensed, it is not necessarily biased: it may be liable to mislead because of what is left out, but omission is not vicious in itself so long as only the relatively trivial and unimportant are omitted. And after all history is not the only form of intellectual activity into which selection enters; most, if not all, works of science are selective too, to say nothing of documents such as reports of royal commissions. Descartes' arguments against the intellectual respectability of history on this head are at best somewhat weak.

It is not mere selection, but selection in accordance with criteria of importance, that the expositor brings into history; and it is on the difference between the notions of importance in history and in science that the difference between history and science turns. Let me attempt to clarify this somewhat oracular pronouncement. A man who compiles a summary statement of the present state of knowledge in some branch of physical theory has to decide what to put in and what to leave out, and he must of course have criteria by which to make the decision. Now to some extent (and here I must qualify the sharp antithesis with which I started) these criteria will depend on what persons he is seeking to enlighten: the selection of material might be different if he were writing for a medical audience, for example, from what it would be if he were addressing students of physics, and it might be different again if he had a special set of physicists (say, theoretical as opposed to experimental physicists) in mind. Yet if you asked such a person why he thought some topic really important, he would always hope to reply that the facts showed it to be. To put the point somewhat crudely, this factor has to be put into a scientific summary while that factor can be omitted because this factor was causally efficacious while that factor was not. To say that something is important in the sphere of natural phenomena is, on this way of putting the matter, to say that its presence or occurrence has far-reaching effects. There are many professional historians who think that a parallel account can be given of importance in history, but I do not think they are correct.

It may help to make my point here if I remind the reader that something can be important either for itself or because of something else which it brings about or to which it is a means. We may call these two concepts, following the parallel usage about 'good', intrinsic and instrumental importance. Now my thesis can be put in the form that both these concepts of importance function in history. If someone says that the French Revolution was the most significant or important event in modern political history he might mean (and perhaps would be commonly taken to mean) that it was the event that had the furthest-reaching and most profound consequences. But his words could be taken in another sense altogether, a sense in which their truth would not depend on the occurrence or non-occurrence of any subsequent happenings: as indicating that the speaker thought the Revolution an event of importance in itself, perhaps as marking a significant manifestation of the free spirit of man. I have heard people speak of the Crucifixion of Jesus Christ as the most important event in Roman history and mean it in this way.

Since it is highly likely that this thesis will be greeted with, at best, polite scepticism, I had better give some further examples. A useful one might be taken from an important change which has come over history-writing in recent years. It is not so very long since history books were filled with the doings of kings and queens, warring nobles and turbulent priests; they tended to concentrate on political and military happenings. Since Marx, or rather since the later years of the nineteenth century, the emphasis has shifted to economic and social history, and the main *dramatis personae* are no longer political figures but, for example, scientists and inventors, whilst the place of the successful monarch as hero of the story has been taken by the common people. What really matters in history, we are told with tiresome frequency, is not eminent persons but the common man. Now I admit that part of the explanation of this shift of interest in historical work is to be found in the growing acceptance of the thesis that economic, as opposed to political, factors are the true determining elements in historical change: the decisions of kings and queens are relatively unimportant in the sense of relatively ineffective, by contrast with economic decisions and developments. But I doubt very much if this is the whole explanation. It is at any rate partly because our estimation of the common man has changed, because ordinary people are no longer regarded as they were in a more aristocratic age, that the common people have come to figure so largely in our histories. Homer had very little to say about the common soldier on either the Greek or the Trojan side, but what he did say about Thersites makes it clear that his silence was not entirely due to the belief that wars were decided by gods and heroes as opposed to common soldiers. We can imagine a modern account of the Trojan War taking a very different form, if only we had the evidence on which to write it.

Other instances of the way in which value judgments have an effect on how we see historical facts might be taken from the history of political institutions, which (at least until recently) we quite naturally assumed should take the form of an account of how our own democratic institutions developed (cf. 'The Evolution of Parliament'), and from the history of ideas, where the emphasis given to ideas we ourselves consider significant (i.e. intrinsically important) is often out of proportion to their causal efficacy (a good recent example would be the interest shown by modern historians of logic in Stoic and medieval anticipations of truth-functional logic). Here again we can readily imagine quite different presentations of the same material, depending on the point of view of the writer. Nor should this fact shock us, as it undoubtedly shocks many professional historians, for it shows only, what we might have been prepared to expect all along, that history is a more complex thing than it is commonly taken to be. It does not show, if I may emphasise the obvious, that history is in no sense a scientific study, concerned to establish what in fact occurred; it most emphatically gives no excuse for thinking that you can build any structure you choose out of the evidence from which historians start. That I take certain things to be intrinsically important in a way only slants my history; it does not determine its details, which remain, on this view as on any other, the main objects of historical scrutiny. But the presence and operation of judgments of intrinsic importance in history seems to me hard to deny, and if this is correct the doctrine of fully scientific history must go by the board, for clearly enough you cannot read such judgments out of the facts.

Why are practising historians so reluctant to accept any such doctrine as that I have put forward? I think there are two main reasons. One is their concern with the minutiae of historical scholarship, which concentrates their attention on the establishment of facts. To many of them, as I have already mentioned, the real stuff of history is to be found in the learned journals, in studies which call attention to new bits of evidence or exploit existing evidence in new ways, rather than in more general books, which they are apt to regard with suspicion, and whose purpose and necessity they do not well understand. But secondly, I think that historians fail to recognise the operation of value judgments in history because they take their own value judgments so much for granted. In Great Britain at any rate, the possibility that there might be any other presuppositions with which one approached history than those which can be broadly described as 'liberal' is simply not considered. The reason for this, no doubt, is that there are few really first-rank historians in the country who do not share liberal views, a fact which reflects the settled political and social conditions in which we live. As a result nonconformist history, of the Marxist variety for example, tends to be technically crude, so much so that it invites no serious interest. It seems to me hazardous to argue from these peculiar conditions that modern British historians fulfil the scientific ideal and operate with no concepts of intrinsic importance. The argument would be similar to that which concluded that *The Times* has no point of view to advance because it calls itself an independent newspaper.

I can think of one way of meeting the case I have put forward without destroying it altogether which historians might find congenial, and I will outline and discuss this before summing up this part of my argument. We can imagine a critic who is ready to grant that, as a matter of fact, historians do make judgments of intrinsic importance, and that they might (or even do) differ in such judgments without its being possible to decide the issue by a simple reference to fact. Nevertheless, such a critic might argue, it does not follow that we cannot find a principle to decide between them rationally, and such a principle is available if we lay it down that one event is more intrinsically important than another if it affects a greater number of people and affects them to a greater extent. As will be obvious, this rather crude formula corresponds to that of the Greatest Happiness principle in morals. Its attraction for historians would be that in effect it resolves a question of value whether it is reasonable to attach intrinsic importance to this or that event—into a question of fact, the question how many people the events concerned affected, and how deep the effect was, and thus makes history scientific after all.

I shall not insist on the vagueness of the phrases just used, or on the difficulties of answering the questions they serve to pose. Nor shall I deny that the suggested criterion might, if it could be rendered suitably specific, have a strong appeal to common sense. What I must emphasise, however, is that the formula cited could not itself claim scientific respectability, or for that matter be objected to on the ground that it is not scientific. As a formula for choosing between judgments of value, it is not itself a simple judgment of value; but equally, and still more obviously, it is not a straightforward statement of fact. You cannot, that is to say, establish its truth by finding out how things are. To subscribe to it is, in effect, to accept a certain moral outlook, the moral outlook of the Utilitarians. I have no wish to deny that this particular outlook often appeals to scientists, particularly social scientists, but this in itself does not make it scientific. If a man refuses to accept this formula, his conduct may be objectionable on various grounds, but not on the ground that he flies in the face of the facts. And it seems to me clear that there are historians, and non-historians too for that matter, who do act as if they rejected this Utilitarian criterion of intrinsic importance.

Let me now try to sum up what I have sought to establish so far. First, I want to say that, while history can be called a science in so far as it possesses recognised and reliable methods for deciding what in particular occurred, this does not, as Bury and most recent professional historians have supposed, mean that it is through and through scientific. The reason for this is that the total picture which it is also the historian's job to construct is not just an aggregate, or function, of particular facts. To say what the Middle Ages were really like you have to do more than recite everything that is known about those times; you have to do more even than give a connected account of medieval life. What you have to do is to present the Middle Ages in perspective, which involves declaring yourself about the significance (intrinsic importance) as well as the instrumental importance of the various facts you assemble. That this is so I connect with the fact that history is always written from a particular point of view, a phrase which includes the acceptance of a certain moral outlook. Though I should not wish to say that we cannot argue about the reasonableness of different possible moral outlooks, and accept or reject them on rational grounds, the fact remains that no definitive ways of choosing between them have yet been discovered. To describe any one such outlook as 'scientific' is to beg the question in its favour.

It would not be correct to argue from the simple circumstance, mentioned earlier, that every historian is what I called an 'expositor', to the conclusion that history is either less or more than a science. That each historian looks at the past from a certain standpoint in time, and that he writes for a particular group of readers—say, Englishmen in the mid-twentieth century as opposed to Germans in the mid-nineteenth—are certainly important in so far as they help to elucidate the otherwise puzzling fact that history is constantly being rewritten; but they are not in themselves a reason for thinking that there is a non-scientific component in history. Mommsen's *History of Rome* may not be all we want today, but if Mommsen differed from his successors only in seeing the events of which he wrote from a different point in space and time the case for scientific history would remain intact, just as it is not affected by the fact that modern Roman historians have (partly through Mommsen's own efforts) more evidence at their command than Mommsen had when he wrote his *History*. Nor is any conclusion of importance to be drawn from the different interests in the past which different historians manifest, except so far as these reveal the presence of something further. Histories of technology can and of course do coexist with histories of literature, and normally the fact that such different accounts of the past are available does not worry any of us. Trouble arises only when we pass from a narrow departmental view and attempt to give something like a rounded picture of an age: it is then that we find ourselves asking whether the invention of tragedy was really as important as, say, the invention of the wheel. Whether we put questions of this sort to ourselves explicitly or no, it is my thesis that answers to them are implicit in the narratives historians offer us, that there is a sense in which they slant, or colour, those narratives from start to finish, and that it is this feature of history about which Bury and his admirers have nothing to say.

It should be noted that I have not said that there is no such thing as truth in history: all I have wanted to urge is that *the* truth about the past is a more difficult concept than most professional historians realise. Of course there are questions which historians ask to which true answers can be given: the whole technical apparatus of the historian remains effective, on my view as on any other. To put the point in the terms I have introduced above, questions about what was instrumentally important admit of true or false answers, and most historians are occupied with these for the greater part of their working lives. One takes it, even so, that even the most dry-as-dust researchers carry out their activities with some thought of a wider synthesis in mind; it is in the construction, or even the mere adumbration, of this that the notion of what is intrinsically important operates. Nor in calling this factor extra-scientific have I wished to give the impression that it is something personal or subjective in any bad sense. I think there *is* a respect in which the personality of the historian is all-important (it is akin to that in which the personality of a novelist is vital: no one else has quite the same grasp and the same vision of the events to be narrated); it was to this among other things that Trevelyan referred when he laid stress on the part which imagination plays in historical work. But seeing the past with certain preconceptions about what was truly important in it is not in any sense a private matter: attitudes of this kind can be, and indeed are, shared by large groups. Again, they can be argued for or disputed, and this too is something which commonly happens. But the argument is not an argument in science or history, since it concerns not merely what is or was the case, but the propriety of a whole attitude to life. If it belongs to any separate discipline, it belongs to philosophy.

The whole of the above case turns on the view that, when an historian sets out to tell us what really happened at some time in the past, or what a particular period was really like, he has to do something more than recite a series of happenings; he has further to help his readers to weigh them up. History is not just description; it is description and assessment. Now I know that this view will not commend itself to many professional historians, and I should like to mention in conclusion some of the considerations which lead me, even so, to think it correct.

Obviously the question has something to do with that of why we study history at all. On this what I shall tendentiously call the official view is clear enough. We study history (or rather historians do) because it is interesting to find things out; men are curious about many things, and amongst others about the past. The motive (or perhaps one should say the one proper motive) for seeking historical knowledge is the simple delight in knowledge for its own sake. That this is part of a true account of the matter I do not wish to deny; that it is the whole of it seems to me very unlikely.

If we ask why people do as a matter of fact take an interest in history, there are doubtless many answers. One very common incentive to historical study is the wish to find out what lies behind, or as we say 'explains', some existing state of affairs which for some reason engages our attention. It is scarcely necessary to emphasise that such an approach is not disinterested, since the curiosity involved is not idle curiosity; it is often connected with some immediate practical purpose. Now it is of course possible to begin a piece of historical study with a practical motive and then to become interested in it for its own sake, pursuing it in far greater detail than practical considerations require; it is this fact which lends the official view such plausibility as it has. But it seems to me that pure curiosity of this sort, though real, is no more than a subsidiary factor in the study of history. If it were the sole motive which impelled people to take an interest in the past, history would hardly occupy the central position in men's thinking which it has today.

Let me try to suggest a sounder view by developing an analogy. We go to foreign countries for a variety of reasons. One very common reason is to do business: we often need to see what foreigners are like, not because we are interested in them for their own sake, but because the knowledge is going to prove practically useful to us. Another very common motive among travellers, especially travellers today, is curiosity: many of us are genuinely anxious to know what goes on in foreign parts, for no other reason than that we find the knowledge diverting. We get pleasure, as people have always done, from seeing and hearing how variegated human nature and behaviour can be. But a mind which confined itself to discovering and noting similarities and dissimilarities in foreign customs and behaviour, no matter how long its owner spent in the countries concerned, would surely be remarkably childlike. Sooner or later with most of us (and sooner rather than

G

later in my own case) sheer curiosity fades out, and we find ourselves watching what goes on around us, not just because the spectacle delights us, but because we need to make comparisons. Seeing how they do it there reminds us of how we do it at home, and the question inevitably arises which practice is the sounder. Not of course that the comparison is ever an easy or a straightforward one: it is only the inexperienced traveller who thinks that you can detach an institution, say the French or American educational system, from the context and background in which it operates and judge it for itself alone. But the difficulty felt here, a difficulty whose existence no honest observer would want to cloak, serves to sharpen rather than diminish interest: the need to make comparisons, to assess both what goes on there and what goes on at home, persists. It is indeed a powerful stimulus to enquiry: the longer we stay in a country, the more we realise that we cannot make a fair judgment without prolonged and serious efforts to find out the facts about it. Factual discovery and assessment thus proceed *pari passu*, and when some shrewd observer comes to write down his experiences in a foreign land they are inextricably mixed.

It seems to me that what is true of foreign travel is also true of history. To go backwards in time is in many ways comparable to going outwards in space, and not least in the circumstance that those who undertake the journey feel the need both to report and to assess.[1] The stories they bring back are not simple descriptions, but what we may call slanted ones: slanted not because they distort facts or deliberately omit them, but because they present them in the light of certain preconceptions which matter to the narrator and to his audience. Such preconceptions do not so much affect what we see (though in unfavourable cases, as we all know, they can have an adverse effect and act as a barrier), as determine to what objects we shall give our attention. What occurred in the past, as every sane person knows, does not depend on what anyone thinks now; how we take it, what we make of it, the construction we put upon it—all these emphatically do. The good historian can no more escape from this fact than can the crudest propagandist,

1. cf. Descartes' *Discourse on Method*, part 1, for this view: 'To hold converse with those of other ages is almost, as it were, to travel abroad; and travel, by making us acquainted with the customs of other nations, enables us to judge more justly of our own.'

though this is no reason for confusing history and propaganda in any other respect.

Confronted with these awkward truths, some historians may wish to retreat to what they would consider a less exposed position. 'All we really know about', we can imagine them saying, 'is how to get the facts. So let us confine ourselves henceforth to saying what the facts were, and leave laymen to judge them.' This amounts to a proposal to eschew general history in favour of the publication of sources, articles and monographs. My difficulties with it are two. First, I do not see exactly how we are to distinguish between monographs and general histories, for every monograph is (I presume) a connected account, and every such account must be written with some wider context in mind, i.e. relative to the historians' point of view. Certainly the author of a monograph may be taken to be addressing his fellow professionals rather than the general public, and this will have an effect on his exposition: it will, for example, result in his posting fewer warning signs to explain the lie of the land to the unwary. But if professional interests diverge from those of ordinary intelligent men, this does not mean that they exclude the latter: historians are human, after all. Secondly, I do not see how on this account of the matter the judging is ever to be done properly. The facts are to be presented—all of them, presumably, or at least as many as can be got, whatever their interest—to persons unfamiliar with them, and they are to be told to make of them what they please. It seems to me that for historians to do this would amount to a serious abdication of responsibility which, if it did not bring their studies into contempt, would at any rate greatly diminish their importance. But I am comforted here by the thought that major historians have never accepted the limited role here sketched for them: they have not hesitated to put the facts into perspective as well as to seek them out, and in so doing have contrived to carry out what Trevelyan rightly saw to be a major task of history, the making men aware of the character of their own time by seeing it in comparison and by contrast with another.

(B)

HISTORICAL CAUSATION

Students and teachers of history are often confused on the subject of historical causation. Their confusion arises out of difficulties experienced at a number of different levels, and my first task will be to give some account of these.

There is first of all the practical difficulty of satisfactorily *identifying* historical causes. To put the matter at its plainest, it is felt that historians ought to be able to say what brought things about as well as what in fact occurred, and yet there is evidently far more disagreement among them in diagnosing causes than in delineating the precise course of events. For instance, we now know a great deal about the diplomatic, political and economic history of the main European powers in the period immediately preceding the first world war, but it would be too much to claim that we know what really caused the war. Was the personality of the German emperor the fundamental factor, as patriotic historians in this country once held, or was it the economic rivalry of the great powers, as their softer-minded successors averred? If someone put down the war to the upsurge of nationalism in Europe, which threatened first the Turkish and then the Austro-Hungarian and Russian empires, thus promising to destroy the whole European balance of power, would he or would he not be obviously wide of the mark? The fact that there are no clear and agreed answers to questions of this sort certainly troubles some students of history. And it seems to me that they are right to be troubled, given the assumption, which is now universal in professional historical circles, that history is a genuine branch of knowledge, a 'science' as Bury called it. What marks off the enquiries we designate as scientific in the broad sense of that term from all others is precisely that their main results command general agreement among all competent persons who engage in them. When Bury said in 1903 that history is a science 'no less and no more' he was undoubtedly claiming that it by that time satisfied this requirement, even if it had not done so in its not very remote literary past. But the claim looks less impressive if it has to be allowed that, as soon as they pass from the course of events to their causes, there is something less than general agreement among historians.

There is a second point about the identification of historical causes which is or can be worrying. It is not only the case that different historians have different answers to such a question as 'What were the causes of the first world war?'; it is also true that the kinds of things selected as historical causes are not always easily comparable. When Mr A. J. P. Taylor argued in *The Origins of the Second World War* that Chamberlain and Daladier were as much to blame for the outbreak of war in 1939 as was Hitler, the issue to be decided was at least a straightforward one, since we can readily compare the effect of Hitler's actions and omissions with those of other statesmen. But when an historian discussing the causes of the first war tells us that the personality of the Kaiser was of small account, the truth being that the essential determining forces in the situation were economic, we do not quite know how to assess what is proffered against what is rejected. The spread of nationalism and the scramble for Africa do not function as causal factors in history on the same level as the institution of the *Entente Cordiale* or a decision to double a naval building programme; to decide whether to accept an account which stresses the first kind of factor as against the second is correspondingly difficult. Nor when it is agreed that what we want in the way of causes is something highly general does everything become plain sailing, for there are rival possibilities at this level too. Nationalist sentiment and the exigencies of the capitalist system agree in being causal factors of a fair degree of abstraction, but that is the only respect in which they do agree. Confronted with alternative histories of Europe in the nineteenth century based respectively on the growth of national selfconsciousness and on developments inherent in the European economic set-up, and asked to choose between them, the average student of history will feel ill-equipped to make the choice. We can imagine him protesting that both sorts of factor were really operative, and trying in consequence to devise a compromise account to do justice to both. But if he were asked to justify his compromise in general terms he would clearly be very unhappy.

These practical difficulties in identifying causes have obviously something to do with unclarity in the historian's mind about *what an historical cause is.* We may suppose that the notion of cause was introduced into history from everyday life, which means that a cause in history was, originally, an event, action or omission but for which the whole subsequent course of events would have been significantly different. The decision of the Emperor William II to dismiss Bismarck in 1890 may serve as an instance of such a cause; it is the sort of thing an examination candidate at a certain level might cite in answer to the question, 'What caused relations between the main European powers to deteriorate sharply in the closing years of the nineteenth century?' Now it is obvious that causes so understood cannot operate in isolation: a cause on this reading is only one of a number of necessary conditions of what is said to be its effect, and can produce the latter only in co-operation with the others. This circumstance is not one that worries us in everyday life where, as Collingwood and others have made abundantly clear, we distinguish causes from conditions (1) according to our interests, and (2) in many cases at least, according to what can in principle be produced or prevented. But historians do not have the same directly practical interest in the past which engineers and doctors have; indeed, we are often told that they have, as historians, no practical interests whatsoever, but are concerned with the past 'for its own sake.' And this means, as it meant for Mill in not dissimilar circumstances, that they can readily develop qualms about the necessary-condition sense of cause. They will pick out a particular feature—say, the character of the German emperor—as decisive in a given situation, and then reflect that it could not have had the effect it did unless all sorts of other things had been true: unless the French had been smarting under defeat and eager for revenge, the British passing through an imperialist phase, and so on. The result is that the common and extremely useful distinction between causes and conditions begins to strike the historian as inadmissible, and a shift is made from necessary to sufficient conditions in his understanding of the term 'cause.' Invited to declare what brought some state of affairs about, he will now proceed to list a wide variety of factors whose joint operation was, in his opinion, sufficient to produce it. But though this move from cause to causes may appear to solve the immediate difficulties, it is clearly far from affording permanent intellectual or even practical satisfaction. When we begin to put down those antecedents of a phenomenon which sufficed to bring it about it is by no means plain what circumstances should be included; every factor we add calls for the addition of further co-operating factors, so that we are threatened with having to say that the causes of *any* historical event must be *all* the events which preceded it. To produce a list of causes for any given historical happening which is at once complete and limited is at the lowest estimate a task of some difficulty. And even if it could be assumed that the problem had been solved in a particular case, it would not follow that the historian would in practice be content to leave the matter there. On the contrary, we might well find him enquiring at the end, with whatever seeming inconsistency, which of the causes named were crucial, which might be said to have been of cardinal importance in bringing about the result and which could be set aside as merely contributory.

This is the point to mention a third source of confusion to historians about historical causes: namely, what philosophers have had to say on the subject. Philosophers of various schools have cast doubt on the propriety of the very notion of an historical cause, or have urged that the term 'cause' can be properly used in historical contexts only when understood in a restricted way. According to Collingwood,[1] for instance, historians, 'unless they are aping the methods and vocabulary of natural science', use 'cause' in a sense in which 'that which is caused is the free and deliberate act of a conscious and responsible agent, and "causing" him to do it means affording him a motive for doing it.' Presumably historians are aping the methods and vocabulary of natural science when they explain historical developments in terms of economic organisation or social structure, or again when they have recourse to the concepts

1. *An Essay on Metaphysics* (1940), pp. 285 ff., and especially pp. 290–5.

of individual or social psychology; if so, Collingwood's pronouncement would prohibit much that we find in existing books of history.
But Collingwood on this subject is moderation itself when com-
pared with Professor Oakeshott, who argues in effect for the
expulsion of the term 'cause' from the whole field of historical
thought and, as if answering Collingwood in advance, describes
Thucydides as 'not only a peculiar, but also a defective historian'
because, for him, 'personal character and motive is a first cause
behind which, as a general rule, he does not press.'[1] To search for
historical causes, in Oakeshott's view, is either to seek to explain
what happens in the historical world by reference to something
entirely outside it ('abstractions like geographical or economic
conditions,' for instance),[2] or it is to break up that world, which
the historian well knows to be an integrated whole, into unreal
fragments, events arbitrarily detached from their background and
falsely thought of as independent existents. Both procedures are
foreign to historical thought proper, the first being imported from
natural science and the second from practical life.

These views of Oakeshott's appear merely paradoxical at first
sight; in fact they are part of a wide-ranging and penetrating
analysis of historical thought and procedure. The thought and
procedure in question are those of the modern 'scientific' historian,
the professional scholar as opposed to the literary amateur; it is to
Maitland that Oakeshott refers most often when he wishes to
document or illustrate his case. Oakeshott professes to set forth
the theory embodied in the practice of scholars like Maitland;
the paradoxes he propounds are, for him, not paradoxes at all, but
conclusions implicit in historical work which is widely admired.
And though he does not claim that his views about causation in
history are explicity advocated by the historians he has in mind, he
has no difficulty in showing that anyone committed to what Bury
described as 'scientific' history must rethink his views about
historical causation. We can plainly make no progress with our
main subject until we have at least glanced at the wider issues here
involved.

1. *Experience and its Modes*, p. 131. This work was published in 1933, but a
later essay of Oakeshott's 'The Activity of being an Historian,' originally published
in 1956 and reprinted in *Rationalism in Politics* (1962), shows that his views about
history have undergone little change. In what follows the two discussions are taken
together.
2. Ibid., p. 132.

The thesis we have to consider is that history is essentially the disinterested study of the past for its own sake. It is not denied that most people most of the time are concerned with the past only so far as it has practical bearing on the present: their curiosity about past happenings and conditions arises out of their present interests and aspirations and is limited to such bits of history as are relevant to these. Nor is it denied that historical thought, even advanced historical thought, is in constant danger of being influenced by practical considerations. As Oakeshott says,[1] we often come across statements in history books which reflect the practical concerns of their authors, statements such as (to use his own examples) 'He dissipated his resources in a series of useless wars' and 'The next day the Liberator addressed a large meeting in Dublin'. But if historians sometimes in fact lapse into practical ways of thinking, we must not suppose that history at its best is anything but cognitive. For the modern scientific historian there is all the difference in the world between the practical past, the past as it lives in the thoughts of the patriot, for example, and the historical past, which is investigated purely for its own sake. The true historian's attitude to the past is in consequence entirely theoretical: he sees his task as being wholly and solely to determine, on the basis of present evidence, what things were like in past times. It would certainly be quite false to suggest that he undertakes this task because he believes that useful results will accrue from its discharge: to think that history will teach a series of lessons is to accept the practical attitude in one of its crudest forms. The truth is rather that the historian loves the past for its own sake, and this means that he treats it as something at once exempt from his influence and entirely without bearing on his present life; not as a living past, but as dead.

Oakeshott deduces various conclusions from this account of the nature of history; the one which concerns us particularly now is that the historian must eschew all expressions which reflect the practical point of view. Earlier exponents of the theory of scientific history (Butterfield, for instance) had protested that it is no part of the historian's task to pass moral judgments. Oakeshott is much more radical, since he wants to get rid of talk about useless wars and the dissipation of resources as well as of bad kings. He argues again that to speak of someone's 'intervening' in an historical situation, or of the death of William the Conqueror as 'accidental', is strictly unhistorical. In history proper nothing is accidental and nobody intervenes, for the historian is concerned solely to find out what occurred and not to do anything about it. True, he hopes at the end of the day to comprehend what happened as well as to say what it was. But he does this not by picking out individual events which were decisive in their sequel, still less by appealing to factors which fall outside history altogether, but by giving what Oakeshott calls[1] 'a complete account of change'. 'In history, *"pour savoir les choses il faut savoir le detail,"* ' and hence history is 'the narration of a course of events which, in so far as it is without serious interruption, explains itself.' By accepting this principle of the 'unity or continuity' of history we find an explanation of historical change 'alternative to that supplied by the presupposition of cause, and free from the defects inseparable from the conception of cause'.[2]

It seems to me that all this amounts not merely to an exposition of the notion of scientific history, but also to its virtual *reductio ad absurdum*. Oakeshott has worked out the consequences of the commonly professed view that history is a purely disinterested study of the past with remarkable logic; to hold that view is indeed to be committed to a complete divorce of the theoretical from the practical, and hence to a renunciation in historical writing of any terms which have practical overtones, including causal terms. But the lesson of this may not be, as Oakeshott apparently supposes, that history is an altogether stranger and far more difficult discipline that the public takes it to be; it could rather be that it is not a purely theoretical study.

I have argued elsewhere[3] that all history (and I should certainly not except modern professional history from this) necessarily contains an extra-scientific component in so far as it is the story of the past, or rather of some part of it, as seen by a particular person at a particular time and presented by him to a particular public. The fact of particularity, if I can call it that, means that each

1. *Experience and its Modes*, p. 143.
2. Ibid., p. 142.
3. See the preceding essay.

historian approaches his task of reconstituting and comprehending the past with his own ideas about what sorts of things in it are intrinsically important, ideas with which he must presume some sympathy in his readers. It is his fundamental judgments of importance which determine to what features of past happenings the historian will give attention. And that such judgments are correct cannot be decided by inspection of the facts, for they are presupposed in anything said about the past. We can find out by consulting the evidence what things in history were important in an instrumental sense, as having far-reaching and far-ranging consequences, but we cannot establish in this way that, for example, what really matters there is the fate of the common man. Nor need this admission lead to the conclusion that all history is irretrievably biased; the proper inference is only that it is all written from a particular point of view. The point of view colours the account the historian gives, or if you like slants it, but it does not (or should not) decide its details. Given that what really matters in history *is* the fate of the common man, there can still be true and false answers to the question how the common man fared at particular times.

Oakeshott would doubtless repudiate this as involving the intrusion of a practical element which is alien to history proper. History as he sees it is written from no point of view whatsoever; it consists of truths which are not merely independent of persons, but independent of any living context of enquiry. Bury had taken the same line when he argued that historians ought to devote themselves to the study of any and every detail of what happened in the past, without regard to the immediate interest of particular periods. His idea was that by accumulating agreed facts we could finally build up a true and timeless account of what the past was really like. I fear that I find this very naïve. 'What the past was really like' is not, as Bury supposed, a function merely of historical evidence, but also of the minds of those who work at the problem of discovering it. Evidence is all-important in history, but so too are the terms in which we address ourselves to it and the general framework of questions inside which we seek to exploit both it and the conclusions we draw from it. And these are presupposed by the historian (normally, of course, in agreement with others), not drawn by him from study of the facts.

There is another, perhaps more controversial, respect in which the doctrine that history is disinterested enquiry into the past seems to me misleading. Oakeshott and those who think with him argue that it is essential to the modern historical attitude that the past be studied without any practical purpose in mind. Now I agree of course that it is the historian's first business to discover truth; I agree too that he must put aside, so far as he can, all prejudices and preconceptions which are avoidable, and let his judgment be guided by what the evidence warrants. But I think all this can be conceded without our having to allow that history is an *exclusively* theoretical activity. Our ultimate purpose in engaging in historical enquiries might not be just to find out the truth about what things were like in former times, but on the basis of that to make some comparison with the present. And I believe that some such purpose does animate our historical studies, and indeed must do if they are to make serious sense. Whatever professional historians may say, historical enquiry is not sustained by mere curiosity; a further motive is involved, namely, the need to find out what past ages were like with a view to making some assessment both of them and of our own times. The past matters to us in the way what foreigners do often matters to us: both can so easily be taken as reflecting on ourselves. In each case to find out if they do we must prosecute more enquiries, get clearer about what was going on then or is going on there. But in neither case is the establishment of fact, or even the understanding of the connexions between facts, the whole object of the exercise.

In the preceding argument my aim has been limited to showing that history, so far from being through and through scientific, should be seen rather as an enquiry pursued in a practical setting and sustained in important respects by practical interests. If I am correct, any account of history which leaves out the practical background of historical studies is bound to be erroneous. So far as I can see the theory of scientific history makes precisely this mistake. It follows that any objection of principle to the use of causal terms in history, on the ground that they belong to the language of action, can be dismissed. As we shall see, the practical component bulks larger in some forms of history than in others: it is very prominent in what may fairly be termed primitive historical writing, and altogether less obvious in the products of the sophisti-cated modern scholar, whose ambition it is to explain historical events at a much deeper level than was attempted by, say, the historians of the ancient world. But the gulf between these two forms of historical activity is perhaps less wide than some modern historians and apologists for history would have us believe.

It may be suggested at this point that Oakeshott's view of history as, in effect, contemplative could have been refuted more quickly and more effectively by simply noting that it is customary for historians, in dealing with their subject-matter, to adopt what recent philosophers have called 'the standpoint of the agent'. To say this is to say that an historian will, wherever possible, narrate or discourse on historical happenings as it were from the inside, trying to present the past, initially at least, as a series of situations and problems encountered by beings who can take cognizance of what is going on and respond accordingly. I think myself that Oakeshott would not agree that this appeal to what we may call the problematic aspect of historical thought really refuted his position, for he would claim that it was characteristic only of pre-scientific history. But now that the limitations of purely theoretical history have been exposed, there seems to be no reason in principle why we should not treat the historian's adoption of a practical standpoint with the seriousness which its prominence appears to demand. In what follows immediately I shall be taking it for granted that much history is an attempt to present the facts from the point of view of the agents concerned, and asking what sense of 'cause' or types of causal question are involved in the carrying out of this task.

First and most obvious, if it is true that the historian presents the persons he writes about as 'conscious and responsible agents', to use Collingwood's phrase, the sense of 'cause' to which Collingwood drew attention will certainly be appropriate in history. Conscious and responsible agents can be caused to do things in the sense that they can be presented with situations or considerations in the light of which they decide to take particular action. The decision in a case of this kind is formally a free one, for though the agent has a motive, and in some instances an overwhelmingly strong motive, for acting as he does, his motive does not compel him to act. An historian may well assume, as we all do in every-day life, that when someone sees his situation as being thus-and-thus, he can be expected to react naturally in such-and-such a manner. But to speak of a *natural* reaction here, as Mr Dray has pointed out, is not just to refer to an established regularity of behaviour; more importantly, it is to speak of behaviour which is judged to be *appropriate*. Hence causes of this first kind are not causes *ab extra*, and to accept them involves no threat to human dignity or rationality.

Collingwood seems to have thought that no other type of causation than the one just mentioned can properly be invoked in history, but here he clearly failed to think out the consequences of his own doctrine that historians are primarily concerned with actions. In adopting the standpoint of the agent, the historian will naturally proceed to at least two other types of causal question. One, in its crudest expression, is the question 'Who caused what?', where the enquirer has two closely connected aims in mind, to fix responsibility and to assess the amount of an agent's contribution to a given end. Fixing responsibility here, it should be noted, is not necessarily a moral matter, though it was treated as largely that by many early historians; it corresponds, as Messrs Hart and Honoré point out in an enlightening discussion,[1] to what a judge does in apportioning liabilities in a civil case rather than to his pronouncing on guilt in a criminal court. And assessing effects is certainly an important historical task, though the causes concerned, in modern historical writing, are no longer always individual persons. Historians can also be interested in the effect of movements, as Mr G. M. Young was when he wrote[2] that he had 'often . . . been perplexed to determine the exact contribution of Puritanism to the middle-class industrial civilisation of England in the nineteenth century', and, for that matter, of natural events, like the silting up of a river. In these cases 'Who caused what?' is widened to 'What caused what?' but the question is still asked in a setting of human activity, since the end towards which the contribution under examination is made is an object of human desire or aversion (as when the silting up of a river leads to a decline in prosperity), or at least of human interest.

A further type of causal question which naturally occurs to anyone who presents history from the inside has already been mentioned in my opening remarks. A man confronting a practical

1. *Causation in the Law;* see especially p. 59 for this type of historical cause.
2. 'Puritans and Victorians' in *Victorian Essays* (1962), p. 62.

problem and finding the outcome not in accordance with his expectations will be led to enquire what caused the situation to turn out as it did. And what he will want here is to put his finger on the particular point at which things began to go wrong (or for that matter to go right), and to identify the circumstance which, from the point of view of the agent concerned, vitally influenced the outcome. A cause in this sense is a necessary condition of some result, picked out from the remaining conditions either because it is something which might have been produced or prevented at will, or because it was in some way unusual or unexpected. Failure to catch a train might cause a man to lose a job in this sense of cause, or unseasonable weather cause a disastrous failure of the crops. This is the concept of causality which Collingwood thought peculiar to the practical sciences, but which is in place wherever and whenever there is a question of there being something to be done. Historians, as we have seen, are inclined to be suspicious of it, partly because of their general confusion about what a cause is, partly because they are seduced by the theory of scientific history into thinking that it is always wrong to read history in terms of purposes contemplated and achieved. But it is one thing to think of history, as the Whig historians are alleged to have done, as all leading up to a certain result, and quite another to present it as a series of problems confronted by the various agents concerned. My point now is that it is with the latter procedure that the necessary condition sense of 'cause' is bound up.

I have expressed all this in a very sketchy manner, but I hope that the points will be clear and sound enough for the purposes of the next step in the argument, which is to suggest that we are now in a position to describe a form of history in which there would be no real problems about historical causation.

Suppose first that history could be taken, in what I shall call the Thucydidean manner,[1] to be exclusively concerned with the doings and sufferings of individuals or groups of individuals, Pericles, Cleon, 'the Lacedaemonians', and so on. Suppose next that, in giving causes of the necessary condition type, the historian were

1. Following here Oakeshott's suggestion (see the quotation on p. 192 above). Thucydides in fact has other characters besides individuals and groups, e.g., 'the people'. And other ancient historians, though otherwise approximating to the model sketched here, bring in further extraneous factors, such as 'the divine element' and 'Fortune'.

always to declare or otherwise make clear from what point of view
he spoke, and were to indicate plainly the ends in which he was
interested. Suppose finally that the three types of cause mentioned
were all recognised as relevant to historical enquiry, that their
compatibility was clearly appreciated, and that no other type of
causal question was allowed in this field. Then there would, in my
view, be no more difficulty of principle in settling problems about
historical causes than there is in settling problems about historical
fact. For I take it, first, that we can sometimes make in history
true statements of the type of which 'His reproaches decided the
minister to make one more attempt' is an instance; we can, that is
to say, assign causes in Collingwood's first sense. The fact that we
cannot question historical personages about their motives does
not debar us in all cases from determining what these were; it
only makes the task more difficult, by depriving us of a source
of evidence. Nor, secondly, do I think that there is any more of
a problem in picking out causes of the necessary condition type
in history than there is in everyday life. To gain conviction we
have admittedly to make our standing in the matter clear, on the
lines already pointed out: we cannot just assume that our point
of view and interests will be immediately recognised, as are those
of, say, a car mechanic in the parallel case. But if we take steps to
satisfy this condition the only remaining difficulty will be whether
we have adequate evidence to make a causal pronouncement, which
is precisely the problem we face when we try to give the bare facts
of what happened. Lastly, determining the efficacy of causal
factors, and thus fixing responsibility, is something which can be
done well or ill in history, just as it can outside it. Not that it is an
easy thing to do well in any circumstances, since the process
involves an activity of isolation and with it a move from the
particular to the general over which mistakes are all too readily
made. And in the case of history there can obviously be no question
of removing a factor to decide what its influence was: the only sort
of experiment that can be carried out is an experiment in the
imagination. But history is not peculiar in this respect, for there
are many occasions in our daily lives where experiment is precluded
but where we nevertheless pronounce with confidence on comparative causal efficacy. It was not possible in 1947, for instance, to
remove Mr Attlee from active politics in order to judge the effect

on his party. But a shrewd observer who had said then that without Attlee to hold them together the Labour Party would break up into mutually hostile groups might now be thought to have spoken with truth.

If someone asked for the *real* cause of an historical event in this simplified form of history, the proper answer would be that there was no cause over and above the several causes given, all of which were necessary and none of which conflicted with any other. No doubt the work of causal diagnosis and assessment could be carried out in greater or less detail, with the result that a less adequate account could sometimes be replaced by one more adequate. But the final aim being to reconstruct and explain the situations depicted as the individual agents saw them, a point could in principle be reached at which it was supposed that *the* answer to each of the types of question had been attained. And in these circumstances to demand a further answer would clearly be absurd.

Contrast now the position in history as we have it. As I see it, there are two principal respects in which the sophisticated history of the present day differs from the primitive history with which we have been concerned, and both have an obvious bearing on the subject of historical causation.

First, in advanced as opposed to primitive history we are occupied with far more than the doings and sufferings of individuals and groups considered as aggregates of individuals, though both continue to play a large part on the historical scene. As well as nations and regions, presented now under single names—'England', 'Europe', etc—as if they had a life, a character and even intentions of their own, institutions and organisations of innumerable kinds come into our histories: the senatorial order, the East India Company, the feudal system, the medieval church may serve as a representative selection. The dramatis personae of history today are thus immensely more numerous and immensely more variegated than were those of history of the Thucydidean variety.

Secondly, these complications connect with a more profound change which renders the impoverished causal apparatus described above quite inadequate for the modern historian. That apparatus was set up on the assumption that in history a number of individual human beings made plans, brought pressure to bear on one another and were checked or favoured by circumstances which might well have been otherwise. No real analysis of the causes at work was called for at this level since, as Oakeshott pointed out, it was not thought necessary to press behind the decisions of individuals in accounting for historical change. The idea was to reconstruct the past as it appeared to the agents concerned, and to give the causes as they saw them. But the ambitions of modern historians certainly go beyond this point. A professional student of history who tackles some perennially interesting subject, such as the Puritan Revolution or the American Civil War, will be expected to do more than provide one more narrative of the main events, together with a statement of their causes as seen by persons alive at the time. He will be expected to point out and display the operation of forces whose significance may well have been overlooked, or at least insufficiently appreciated, by those on whose lives they impinged, and in this way to offer some analysis of the factors which caused things to work out as they did. The forces in question are those exerted by, for instance, the more or less permanent political or economic conditions in which men had to act in the periods under investigation; and justification for bringing them in is to be found in the reflection that such forces clearly influence what men do, if only by restricting the range of choices open to them. But there is another aspect of the matter which is of great importance in this connexion. As well as being limited by the background against which they act, the activities of human beings owe many of their special characteristics to the fact that they are social activities, undertaken not by individuals acting in isolation but by beings who are members of organisations of every degree of complexity, the nature of which they have for the most part to take for granted (it is seldom if ever alterable by *individual* decision) and the opera-tion of which often seems to proceed by a logic of its own. Modern historians differ from their less sophisticated predecessors, among other things, in being altogether more conscious of the social dimension of action. They have grasped the all-important fact that men appear on the stage of history in a variety of rôles, and that what they do as, for instance, princes of the church, officers in the revolutionary army or members of the propertied classes is not entirely of their own choosing, but is determined, often to a very significant extent, partly by ways of proceeding which are commonly accepted, partly by what others concerned in the activity do or are expected to do. And they realise that no piece of historical exegesis can claim to be adequate unless it does justice to these facts.

But though modern historians are thus sensitive to the operation in history of forces of which their predecessors were all but unaware, it cannot be said that they have very clear ideas about the sort of causes these forces are. As we saw at the beginning, some of them are uneasy about the relationship between the parts of history where reference is made to such things as social structure and national aspirations and the parts which are written in terms of the actions of individuals. Others feel unhappy at the whole idea of the historian's invoking impersonal factors as historical causes, on the ground that this at once sells the pass to social science and involves a commitment to determinism which is quite foreign to the normal historical attitude. Nor when it is allowed that the historian must appeal to further sorts of cause than those which function at the personal level is there any agreement on how to assess claims to have presented such causes correctly. In short, all the main perplexities about historical causation, except those which are due to uncritical acceptance of the notion of scientific history, are connected with the aspiration of the modern historian to offer a deeper analysis of the course of events than traditional historians attempted. A full discussion of this procedure is obviously called for if those perplexities are ever to be cleared up.

In the remainder of this essay I can contribute only a few preliminary notes for such a discussion. I want to say, first, that to speak of history as shaped by economic necessities or determined by social structure is not necessarily to exclude an account of it in terms of personalities. General causes of the former kind should normally be taken as supplementing particular causes, not as ruling them out of court. That this is so we can see from an instance. If a student of recent history were given the task of accounting for the collapse and virtual disappearance of the Liberal party in Britain between the two wars, we should expect him to say something about the electoral system of the country, which made it difficult if not impossible for more than two parties to survive, and again about the harsh economic climate of the time, which drove voters to throw in their lot either with the party pledged to preserve existing property relations or with the party whose object was to alter them radically. We might even find him saying that, in these conditions, the elimination of the Liberals as a serious political force was inevitable. But this would not mean that he omitted all reference to persons in his account. Lloyd George and Asquith would come into his story as they would have done in a less sophisticated historical age; they might even fill the foreground as Pericles and Cleon filled the foreground in the pages of Thucydides. The difference would be that we should see, as we do not see in Thucydides, that such persons are not the fully independent agents they generally take themselves to be; we should see that these two men in particular had to act in a framework which was not of their own choosing, or indeed of any single person's choosing, and whose very existence prevented their attaining many of the ends they set themselves. By thus bringing in a reference to the background of action the historian would reveal standing conditions which shaped the course of events in significant ways. But he would not be saying that they were solely responsible for what occurred, since they clearly functioned not as efficient but only as formal causes.

I do not wish to deny that a clear grasp of the importance of the kind of causal factor I have in mind would have the effect of reducing our estimate of the significance of individuals in history. As I see it, such a reduction is clearly called for: we have too long considered individual actions apart from the context in which they take place, more particularly the social context. But it would be quite wrong to take this as implying commitment to historical determinism. To say that the fact that the working classes were by then relatively well organised on the industrial side precluded the Liberals from making a come-back in 1929 is not to argue that history is made by 'vast impersonal forces', to use Sir Isaiah Berlin's famous phrase. What is objectionable in such forces is, presumably, that no human being can do anything about them: they operate whether we like it or not, with the supposedly ineluctable necessity of the law of gravity. But though trade unions were neither created nor can be destroyed by single individuals, and though once created they function independently of persons, in so far as their very structure and organisation dictates the mode of their operation, it is not of course true that they cannot be altered by human effort, even if that effort has got to be collective.

Nor is it true again that their existence robs those concerned of *all* freedom of choice, though it may remove just the particular liberties which some men would like to have; the liberty to take on and dismiss workers at will, for instance, or to pay them just enough to keep above starvation level.

This account may still be viewed with suspicion, especially by historians of the more conservative sort, in view of what is said about institutions operating with a logic of their own: the apparent implication being that they function in virtue of possessing a particular *type* of structure, some *general* knowledge of which may reasonably be demanded in the persons who talk in terms of them. This is to make history dependent on the conclusions of the social sciences, when many historians think that, so far from being necessary for their work, these conclusions are totally irrelevant to it. On this I have two comments to offer. First, that the implication stated above is not in fact a clear one: historians could, if they chose, continue to think in terms of particular cases, and get the generality needed by always keeping a plurality of similar cases in mind. They would then be, and indeed perhaps mostly are, like doctors with wide experience but no knowledge of theory. But, secondly, I suggest that suspicion of theory by historians has been taken to absurd lengths, and that it depends, in part at least, on mistaken notions of what theory can provide. We should not look to the social sciences (or even to the physical sciences) to supply us with general truths which will apply unequivocally to every concrete instance that comes up, nor should we dismiss them as worthless if they do not meet this requirement. A study of this kind can be enlightening even if, and indeed just because, it abstracts from actual circumstances and considers only what happens in 'pure' cases. The results of such a study cannot be immediately applicable, but that is not to say that they are not applicable at all. And that they can have application even in the sphere of history is shown by the fact that economic historians have been able to make use of the conclusions of pure economics, an abstract discipline if ever there was one.

I have so far said nothing on the question how we are to choose between historical accounts of the sophisticated modern type which cite different kinds of background factor, or which stress the factors they adduce in different ways. This is, in my view, much the hardest of the problems about historical causation with which I began this discussion, and I fear I can do little towards solving it now. I am inclined to think that if historians were more familiar with the theories from which they took their analytical concepts they might prove in practice both more confident and more adept in handling them, and so better at choosing between alternative sets. Theoretical study could at least sharpen insight into the interconnections of such a set of ideas, and in so doing enable the historian to appreciate their proper explanatory force. But I also want to suggest that part of the difficulty here, as was the case with the more primitive types of historical causation we considered earlier, may arise from the prevalence of the notion that history is respectable only if written from no point of view. The answer to the man who wonders whether the right way to see nineteenth-century European history is in terms of national aspirations or of economic necessities may well be to ask him to declare his interests. The two sorts of history, in other words, could well be complementary rather than alternatives. Historians so far have perhaps been precluded from accepting this line because of their commitment to the notion of general history, an idea which is widely accepted but which all the same seems to cry out for critical scrutiny. But I hope I shall be forgiven if I do not embark on any such scrutiny here.

NOTE ON BOOKS FOR FURTHER READING

1. *General*

The main problems of critical philosophy of history are discussed at an advanced level in Morton White's *Foundations of Historical Knowledge* and A. C. Danto's *Analytical Philosophy of History*, both published in 1965. Danto has a chapter exploring the conceptual difficulties of 'substantive', i.e. speculative, philosophy of history. William Dray's *Philosophy of History* (1964) is a short but sophisticated introduction to both sides of the subject. W. B. Gallie's *Philosophy and the Historical Understanding* (1964) stresses the narrative element in history interestingly. Among older books the reader should not miss Collingwood's *Idea of History* (1946; Ed. T. M. Knox), which is always challenging if not always satisfying. He should also consult the writings of Dilthey (conveniently excerpted in H. P. Rickman's *Meaning in History*, 1961) and Croce, as well as Bradley's early essay *The Presuppositions of Critical History* (1874; reprinted in *Collected Essays*, vol. I, 1935).

Extracts from Dilthey, Croce and Collingwood, together with the main speculative philosophers of history and some contemporary writers, are given in P. Gardiner's useful anthology *Theories of History* (1959). Fritz Stern's *The Varieties of History* (1956) complements this by including extracts from some of the classical historians about the nature and methods of history. For recent pronouncements by historians see especially Marc Bloch's *The Historian's Craft* (E.T., 1949) and E. H. Carr's lively *What is History?* (1961).

2. *Critical Philosophy of History*

Historical explanation has been extensively discussed in recent years.

Statements of the 'idealist' view mentioned in Chapter 2 are to be found in Dilthey and Collingwood, op. cit.; for an acute discussion of Collingwood's position see A. Donagan, *The Later Philosophy of R. G. Collingwood* (1962). The classical statement of the 'positivist' thesis is Carl Hempel's 'The Function of General Laws in History' (1942; text in Gardiner's *Theories of History*), though K. R. Popper claims to have originated the theory. For Popper's views see his *The Poverty of Historicism* (1957). P. Gardiner in *The Nature of Historical Explanation* (1952) offers a modified version of the positivist theory; W. Dray in *Laws and Explanation in History* (1957) criticises this and reconstructs the idealist view. Isaiah Berlin in 'The Concept of Scientific History', in *History and Theory*, 1960, is also sympathetic to idealism. For further developments in the controversy see *Philosophy and History, a Symposium*, Ed. S. Hook (1963), with contributions by Dray and Hempel, among others.

Hook's volume can also be consulted on historical objectivity, as can the works cited by White and Danto, with J. W. Meiland, *Scepticism and Historical Knowledge* (1965). On causation in history there is a good chapter in White and some brief but useful comments in H. L. A. Hart and A. M. Honoré, *Causation in the Law* (1959).

3. *Speculative Philosophy of History*

Of the classical writers discussed or referred to in this volume there are English translations of Vico's *New Science* by T. G. Bergin and Max Fisch; Kant's essay 'Idea for a Universal History' by L. W. Beck in *Kant on History* (1963); Hegel's *Philosophy of Right* §§ 341–60 are relevant) by T. M. Knox, and his *Lectures on the Philosophy of History* by J. Sibree; Comte's *System of Positive Policy*, vol. III, by E. S. Beesly and others. There is also an old translation of Herder's *Ideas*.

Historical information about this type of theorising is to be found in J. B. Bury's *The Idea of Progress* (1920) and in F. E. Manuel's *Shapes of Philosophical History* (1965). On particular writers the following are especially useful: on Vico, the introduction to his *Autobiography* by T. G. Bergin and Max Fisch; on Kant, Beck, op. cit. and E. L. Fackenheim in *Kantstudien*, 1956–7; on Hegel, W. Kaufmann: *Hegel* (1965); on Comte, H. B. Acton: 'Comte's Positivism and the Science of Society', *Philosophy*, 1951. Acton also has an excellent discussion of Marx on history in *The Illusion of the Epoch* (1955). For further light on Marx see S. Hook, *Towards the Understanding of Karl Marx* (1934; with appendix containing four letters on historical materialism by Engels) and M. M. Bober, *Karl Marx's Interpretation of History* (1927).

On Toynbee see the essays and reviews collected by M. F. Ashley

Montagu in *Toynbee on History* (1956), together with Toynbee's replies to his critics in vol. XII of his *Study*, 'Reconsiderations'. On Spengler see H. S. Hughes, *Oswald Spengler* (1952). Among theological writers on history the following are especially notable: H. Butterfield, *Christianity and History* (1949); Reinhold Niebuhr, *Faith and History* (1949); R. Bultmann, *History and Eschatatology* (1957); see also A. Richardson, *History, Sacred and Profane* (1964) for general comment. The logical problems involved in attempts to discover laws or trace patterns in history are discussed in Popper, op. cit. and in I. Berlin, *Historical Inevitability* (1954).

INDEX